Systems in Motion
Exploring Complexity through an Interdisciplinary Lens

LEVEL C

Part of a three-level series

Level A (for ages 5 and up)

Level B (for ages 8 and up)

Level C (for ages 13 and up)

by Jennifer Andersen and Anne LaVigne
in collaboration with the Creative Learning Exchange

Creative Learning Exchange
Acton, Massachusetts
2014

DEDICATION

To Jay Forrester
for his tireless commitment to making the world a better place
through empowering young people to better understand the complexity around
them and make a positive difference in their own and others' lives.

ACKNOWLEDGEMENTS

This book was created through the efforts, encouragement, and
support of many and is the culmination of learning gained from years of
collaboration with more people than we could possibly name. In addition to
being grateful to our loving families and to each and every person who
helped us along the journey, special thanks goes to those directly
involved in the review, editing, and final project completion:

Jan Bramhall
Joanne Egner
Marcy Kenah
Bunny Lawton

Michael Radzicki
George Richardson
Amanda Wait

Funding was made possible through the generosity of Jay Forrester.

Table of Contents

Getting Started — 7

    Introduction — 9

    Simulations and Lessons — 9

    Implementation Guidelines — 10

    Materials and Logistics — 11

Simulations and Lessons — 13

Level C Lessons (for ages 13 and up)

    Springs Everywhere: Exploring Spring-Mass Dynamics — 15

    Romeo and Juliet – In Rapturous Oscillation? — 31

    Rabbits, Rabbits, and More Rabbits: Logistic Growth in Animal Populations — 47

    Waves of Change: Predator and Prey Dynamics — 61

    Eat and Be Eaten: Prey as Predator, Predator as Prey — 77

    The Big Squeeze: Pressure, Achievement and Burnout — 95

    Hog Wild: Fluctuations in Commodities Markets — 117

Everything Else — 133

    Appendix A: Characteristics of Complex Systems — 135

    Appendix B: System Dynamics Visual Tools — 137

    Appendix C: Technical Matters — 138

Getting Started

"Every thought tends to connect something with something else, to establish a relation between things. Every thought moves, grows and develops, fulfills a function, solves a problem."

Lev S. Vygotsky, *Thought and Language*

PHOTO BY ANNE LAVIGNE

Introduction

This series of seven interdisciplinary lessons with accompanying free, online simulations has explicit connections to curriculum content standards and to critical thinking skills.

Simulations also illustrate how perceived problems or undesirable behavior can arise from the structure of a system itself, as opposed to outside influences. A system with many ups and downs behaves in that manner because it has an inherent tendency to do so. For example, the very nature of a spring is to bounce up and down, not due to some outside force, but because its structure causes it to do so.

Simulations and Lessons

Each simulation creates an open, engaging environment for students to explore guided and self-generated questions, while gaining content knowledge.

Level of the materials

Most simulation contexts have three levels – A, B, and C. These levels correspond, in general, to different ages:

Level A – Ages 5 and up
Level B – Ages 8 and up
Level C – Ages 13 and up

In addition, since the levels share the same underlying context, a teacher may find using different levels appropriate for differentiation of instruction.

This book contains only the Level C lessons and handouts, other books in the series include materials for the other two levels, A and B.

Connections to curriculum standards

Although the lesson contexts may initially seem focused on a particular subject area, each of the simulations relates to curriculum standards across multiple contexts. The table on the next page (Figure 1) illustrates simulation contexts, available levels, and curricular connections.

Lesson Context	Description	Levels A	B	C	Engineering	Language Arts	Math	Science	Social Studies	Social/ Emotional
Spring	See how a spring (e.g., a Slinky®) moves when changing its structure and environment.	√	√	√	√	√	√	√		
Relationships	Explore relationships on the playground (A) and in literature (B and C)	√	√	√		√	√	√	√	√
Population	Watch animal populations increase up to a limiting carrying capacity.	√	√	√		√	√	√		
Predator/Prey	Investigate a relationship between predator and prey populations, based on a real island ecosystem.	√	√	√		√	√	√		
Predator/Prey/ Food	Take on the role of wildlife manager to see how the availability of food for prey affects the whole system.	√	√	√		√	√	√		
Burnout	Become a peer advisor, helping students find solutions to burnout cycles.		√	√		√	√	√	√	√
Commodities	Write an article as a journalist investigating different farming practices, while learning about commodity cycles.		√	√		√	√	√	√	

FIGURE 1: Simulations and Context Connections

Implementation Guidelines

These are general guidelines for using the simulations with accompanying lessons and handouts. Each lesson includes suggestions for introducing, implementing, debriefing, and assessing a simulation. Teachers are free to adapt the materials for their own use to meet the needs of their students.

Level of guidance

The simulations allow students to work interdependently with a partner, while following prompts on the screen and within the handouts. Depending on individual and class needs, the teacher may need to provide additional whole-class or small group guidance throughout the simulation experience.

Omit some or all of the handouts, based on instructional goals and depending on student age, reading ability, and level of self-direction. One option is to create a flexible, more 'organic' environment for students to explore the simulations, along with alternate methods for students to demonstrate understanding.

Making predictions and comparing results

The use of dynamic simulations opens possibilities for students to make predictions, design simple experiments, and compare actual results to predicted behavior. These tasks are connected to multiple curricular standards and also enhance students' ability to think deeply about what is causing particular results. The handouts guide students through this process, but conversations before and after the simulation can help students practice the critical thinking skill of evaluating interdependent relationships within a dynamic system.

Assessing student learning

Assessment can take place informally through small group/class conversations and formally through simulation handouts, independently completed written assessments, and oral presentations.

Informal assessment: As students work through the simulations, observe the kinds of conversations they have. For example, to what degree are they able to describe cause-and-effect connections among the parts? For this reason, having students work within a group of 2–3 students encourages collaborative decision-making and reflection as they experience simulation results. While 'floating' through the classroom to observe student progress, ask students open-ended questions about discoveries and insights gained.

Formal assessment: The lessons include handouts, assessments, and suggested projects. Although example student responses for some handout questions are included within lesson plans, no official answer keys are provided. Most questions allow for multiple "correct" answers. Some questions seek an opinion, inference, or interpretation, along with evidence. These questions, by their very nature, do not lend themselves to the creation of a discrete set of answers.

Materials and Logistics

Very little, in terms of supplies, preparation, and materials is needed for implementation.

Printing the handouts

Unless otherwise indicated, handouts are formatted for double-sided printing. Some handouts are optional, depending on prior student experience. For example, one lesson includes a handout based on having read a particular book.

Materials

All that's needed are one or more computers with Internet access and the lessons with accompanying handouts. At the time of this printing, the simulations will not work on iPhone or iPad devices unless a separate flash-capable browser app is purchased and installed. They will work on many other portable tablets. *Note*: if only one computer is available, one option is to project the simulation and use it as a whole-class activity/discussion. For each run, ask students to propose settings, run the simulation, and discuss as a class.

Accessing the simulations

All simulations are available online at no cost from The Creative Learning Exchange via the QR code or at:

https://exchange.iseesystems.com/profile/25/52

Time

Each lesson gives a general guideline for completion time, generally three to four 45-minute class periods to introduce, use the simulation, and debrief the experience. The actual time needed to complete any particular simulation will vary based on individual and classroom differences. Feel free to adjust the amount of time, based on instructional goals.

Last word

How easy is this…really? It's just as simple as opening the link to one of the simulations. The handouts can guide students, so they don't miss parts of the simulation content, but students can also gain new insights through a more organic exploration of the simulations. No one right way exists to use these resources. Explore, discover, and enjoy together with your students!

Simulations & Lessons

"The intuitively obvious 'solutions' to social problems are apt to fall into one of several traps set by the character of complex systems."

Jay W. Forrester, *World Dynamics*

Lesson 1 – Level C

Springs Everywhere: Exploring Spring-Mass Dynamics

Overview

The spring simulation allows students to experiment with a virtual spring-mass system. They can change settings, run the simulation, and compare results. The default simulation behavior is equilibrium, as the spring is initially at rest. By changing the settings, a variety of oscillatory behaviors are generated. This model is intended as an introduction for this series of oscillatory models, although it also aligns with specific math and science curricular standards.

Learning Goals

- Represent, interpret, and compare data on a graph.
- Explain concepts including oscillation, equilibrium, position, spring constant, mass, force, momentum, and resistance.
- Represent the system's loop structure, showing how position and momentum impact one another.
- Describe how and why springs oscillate.

LESSON 1 – LEVEL C – AGES 13+

Time
Two or three 45-minute sessions

Materials
- One computer for every 2–3 students
- Handouts (See pages 19–29)

Curricular Connections
- Science: ...use many models, including physical objects, plans, mental constructs, mathematical equations, and computer simulations.
- Science: Laws of motion are used to calculate precisely the effects of forces on the motion of objects.
- Math: Look for and make use of structure, and interpret functions that arise in applications in terms of the context*

Common Core State Standards

Key system dynamics concepts and insights
- The structure of a spring system creates an oscillation.
- Oscillatory behavior can occur both within physical systems, e.g., a spring and within social systems, e.g., relationships.

Additional information

FIGURE 1: Title Screen

Student Challenge

Create a variety of springs that produce specific behaviors. Be able to discuss what is causing the variations in oscillatory behavior.

Lesson Details

Preparation

1. Create groups of 2–3 students each.
2. Check computers to make sure you can access the online simulation.
3. Copy handouts for each student. See the chart below to determine how many copies of each handout you'll need.

#	Page	Handout	Description	Copies
1	19–22	Introduction with Baseline Runs	Students get started with the simulation using step-by-step directions.	Copy single-sided. 1 copy per student
			They then set up and record the data from a baseline run for the spring.	Copy double-sided. 1 copy per student
2	23–24	Experimental Run	Students explore "What if?" questions, recording their data for each run. A minimum of three runs is recommended.	Copy double-sided. 3+ copies per student, depending on how many runs you'd like students to do.
3	25–27	Debrief	Students step through the debrief and write their reflections.	Copy double-sided. 1 copy per student
4	28	Assessment	Students summarize their learning.	Copy single-sided.
5	29	Assessment (Optional)	Students define spring concepts and describe interdependencies.	Copy single-sided.

4. *Optional:* You may want to read the background information about the underlying structure of the model. This can be useful as you guide students to understanding the model behavior, as it relates to real world behaviors, and the limitations of the model. (Spring-Mass Model Background Info available as a separate file http://www.clexchange.org/ftp/documents/x-curricular/CC2012_Oscillations1BackgroundInformation.pdf)

Lesson Sequence

1. If available, you can have students experiment with real springs, such as a Slinky®. By observing the behaviors of real springs, students can compare that experience to the theoretical output of the simulation.

2. Introduce students to any specific content knowledge related to springs. This may include concepts such as oscillation, equilibrium, position, spring constant, mass, force, momentum, and resistance. Discuss the difference between an initial position of a spring and the current position, once the spring is released.

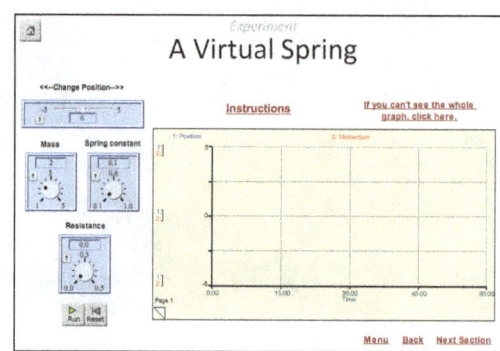

FIGURE 2: Control Panel

3. Have students open the simulation and work through the simulation introduction, and experiments using the guided handouts. Note that the handouts guide students through the simulation in a step-by-step manner. If you'd like to leave the exploration more open, then you may eliminate some of the handouts. Figure 2 shows the control panel screen.

Debrief and Assessment

1. Have students use the debrief handouts to reflect on the simulation experience. You can also debrief the simulation experience as a class, using ideas for bringing the lesson home. The assessments on pages 28 and 29 check for basic understanding of spring concepts embedded within the simulation.

2. General answers for the assessment on page 28:

   Graph 1: Initial position = 0

   Graph 2: Initial position = 5, low spring constant, low mass, no resistance.

   Graph 3: Initial position = 5, high spring constant, low mass, no resistance.

   Graph 4: Initial position = 5, low spring constant, low mass, high resistance.

3. Possible response for assessment on page 29: As the spring position rises toward 0 and eventually crosses to a positive position, the displacement goes down toward 0 and eventually crosses the 0 line to a negative displacement. As displacement falls, the impulse continues moving from a +1 to a -1, causing momentum to rise. As the momentum increases, velocity also increases, thus causing the position to rise. When the spring has reached its highest position, the system reverses itself with position now falling and displacement rising from a negative number to a positive number, and so on. Eventually, all the graphs reach equilibrium because of resistance.

Assessment Ideas

Have students use the debrief and assessment handouts.

The debrief takes students step-by-step through the debrief screens. The assessment checks whether students understand how the basic structure of the spring system generates particular behavior patterns.

Bringing the Lesson Home

- Discuss these and any other questions that have surfaced about model behaviors.
- What causes the spring to oscillate?
- What causes the spring to come to a resting point?
- What caused faster oscillations? Slower? Highest? Lowest?

ACKNOWLEDGEMENTS

Lesson 1 – Level C • Springs Everywhere: Exploring Spring-Mass Dynamics
©2014 Creative Learning Exchange

This model is one in a series of models that explores the characteristics of complex systems.

Model created with contributions from Jennifer Andersen, Anne LaVigne, Mike Radzicki, George Richardson, Lees Stuntz, with support from Jay Forrester and the Creative Learning Exchange.

Image Sources and Credits

The following images are in the public domain:

Lotus suspension - Source: http://commons.wikimedia.org/wiki/File:Lotus_18_suspension_detail.jpg; author Duke le palois

Trampoline - Source: http://en.wikipedia.org/wiki/File:Hometrampoline.jpg; author Ludraman

English longbow - Source: http://en.wikipedia.org/wiki/File:Englishlongbow.jpg; author James Cram; public domain

Pocket springs - Source: http://en.wikipedia.org/wiki/File:Pocket_springs.jpg; author Ankathebest

Mensa connections - Source: http://commons.wikimedia.org/wiki/File:Mensa_Connections.JPG; author Fitzftz

Vertical spring-mass system - Source: http://en.wikipedia.org/wiki/File:Simple_harmonic_oscillator.gif; author Oleg Alexandrov

The following images are used under the Creative Commons Attribution-ShareAlike 3.0 Unported license (http://creativecommons.org/licenses/by-sa/3.0/deed.en) on either Wikipedia.org or Wikimedia Commons:

Coil spring - Source: http://en.wikipedia.org/wiki/Image:Springs_009.jpg

Compression spring - Source: http://commons.wikimedia.org/wiki/File:CompressionSpring.jpg; author Taktoa

Rubber bands - Source: http://en.wikipedia.org/wiki/File:Rubber_bands_-_Colors_-_Studio_photo_2011.jpg; author Bill Ebbesen

Bicycle - Source: http://en.wikipedia.org/wiki/File:Cannondale_Headshok.jpg; author Andrew Dressel

Front page bungee - Source: http://commons.wikimedia.org/wiki/File:Bungee_jauntal_1.jpg; author Gerhard Grabner

Earth - Source: http://commons.wikimedia.org/wiki/File:Earths.jpg; author Stephen Slade Tien

Millennium Bridge damper - Source: http://en.wikipedia.org/wiki/File:London_Millennium_Bridge_-_Damper_beneath_deck,_north_side_-_240404.jpg; author Tagishsimon

The following image is used under the Creative Commons Attribution-Share Alike 2.5 Generic license (http://creativecommons.org/licenses/by-sa/2.5/deed.en)

Internet sign - Source: http://commons.wikimedia.org/wiki/File:Internet-Sign.jpg; author cawi2001

The following image is used under the Creative Commons Attribution 2.0 Generic license (http://creativecommons.org/licenses/by/2.0/deed.en) on Wikimedia Commons:

Bungee jumper into water - Source: http://commons.wikimedia.org/wiki/File:Bungee_jumping_-_Kawarau_Bridge,_New_Zealand-15Jan2010.jpg; author Matthias Klappenbach

LESSON 1, LEVEL C, HANDOUT 1 – P.1

Springs Everywhere – Introduction

Open web address: http://www.clexchange.org/curriculum/complexsystems/oscillation/
Select the "Springs Everywhere: Exploring Spring-Mass Dynamics Level C simulation" and click, "Start."

You'll explore the sections (in **bold**) as indicated. Remember, you can always revisit a section anytime you like.

1. Click Introduction – Spring Dynamics
a. List at least five examples of how springs are used.

b. What does the phrase, "form ever follows function," mean to you?

c. What is at least one specific example of "form follows function?" You can give an example from architecture, mechanics, biology, or another context.

Click Menu. Click Experiment with the Model.
d. Click on the "?" for each of the settings and then define these in your own words.

Change Position:

Mass:

Spring Constant:

Resistance:

You will use the following worksheets to predict and record your virtual experiments.

LESSON 1, LEVEL C, HANDOUT 1 – P.2

Run # 1: Baseline Runs for Spring

Click on the ? for each of the sliders and dials to see what each one does. Input the values shown below onto the simulation screen, but don't run it yet.

Change Position	0
Mass	2
Spring Constant	0.1
Resistance	0

Predict: What do you think will happen to the spring's position over time?

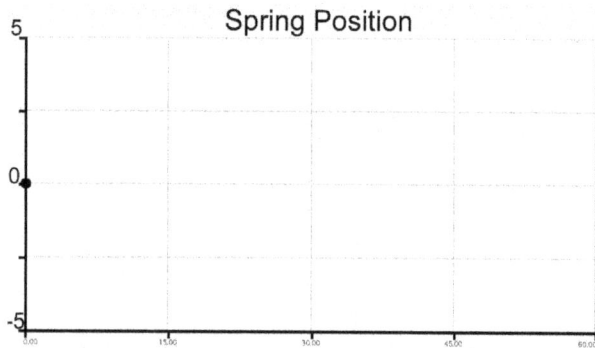

Draw a general prediction as a line on the graph. Note that the spring will start at a position of '0' which is at the dot shown on the y-axis. Now **click** "Run."

Analysis: What actually happened? Using two colors, create a key, show the scale on the y-axis, and draw the graphs for the spring's position and momentum. Note that because this run shows equilibrium, the line for momentum overlaps the line for position, which also stays at '0' for the entire run. You can see these individually by clicking the tab at the bottom left corner of the graph. You'll also see graphs for velocity, impulse, and displacement. Don't worry about these extra graphs.

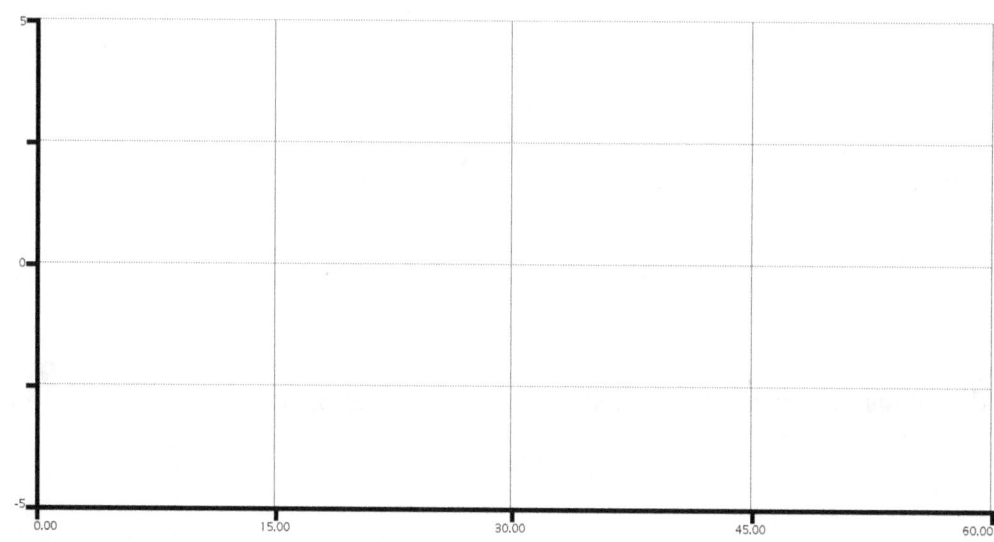

20 • LESSON 1 – Level C • Springs Everywhere

Baseline Run (continued)

a. Explain your results. Why was the spring in equilibrium?

b. What one setting would you need to change from the current settings to get the spring moving?

c. Why would this work?

Make that one change and then run the simulation again. If you get the spring to go out of equilibrium, then record your results below in the table and on the graph as before. If not, then go back to 'b' and 'c' above and revise your answers.

Change Position	
Mass	
Spring Constant	
Resistance	

Don't forget to make a key!

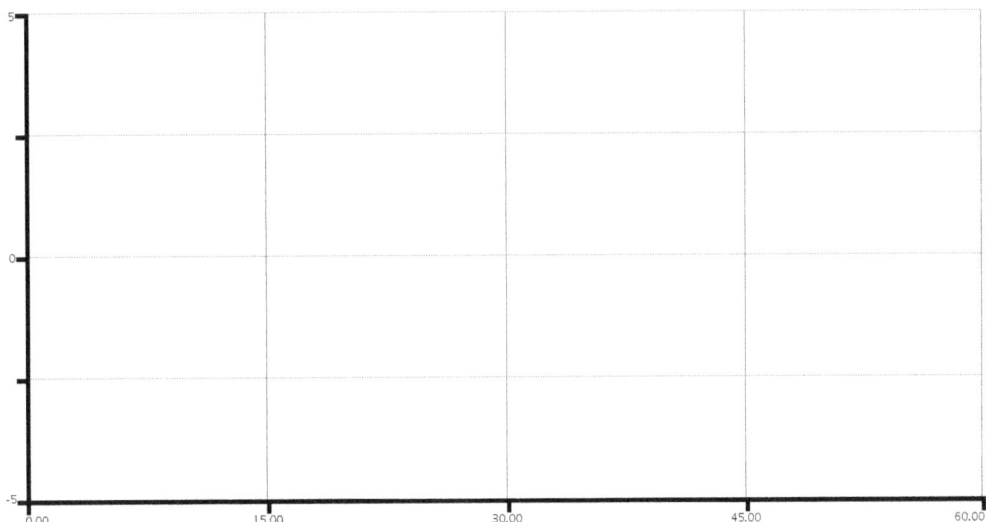

Baseline Run (continued)

d. Approximately how much time does it take for the spring to go through one cycle? (*Hint:* on the position graph, look at the time distance between two peaks. You can click and hold on the graph line to see the values.)

e. What do you think is impacting the speed of the oscillation cycle?

f. Why does the spring appear to oscillate forever?

g. Continue your exploration, asking "What if" questions. Ask one question at a time and then record what happens on a new run sheet.

   Question 1: What might happen if the spring had a heavier mass?

   Question 2: What might happen if the spring had a higher spring constant?

   Question 3: What might happen if the spring was impacted by resistance?

   Question 4: What might happen if the initial position of the spring was set differently?

   Question 5: What are some other questions you could explore? Write one or more questions below and try them one at a time.

LESSON 1, LEVEL C, HANDOUT 2 – P.1

Springs Everywhere – Experimental Run

Run #: _____ **Question:** _____

Make sure to change only the position (to a number other than 0) and one other setting from the baseline values that relate to your question.

Change Position	
Mass	
Spring Constant	
Resistance	

Predict: What do you think will happen to the spring's position over time?

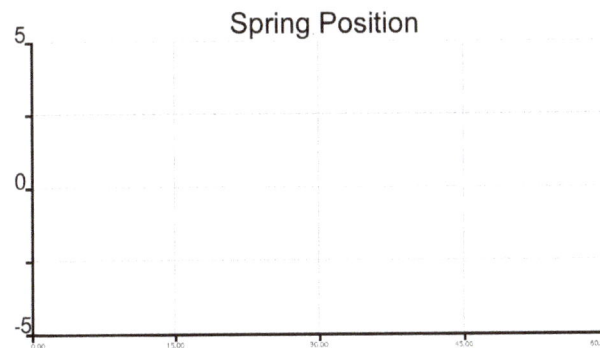

Draw a general prediction as a line on the graph. Note that the spring will start on the y-axis at whatever position you set above. Now **click** "Run."

Analysis: What actually happened? Using two colors, create a key, show the scale on the y-axis, and draw the graphs for the spring's position and momentum.

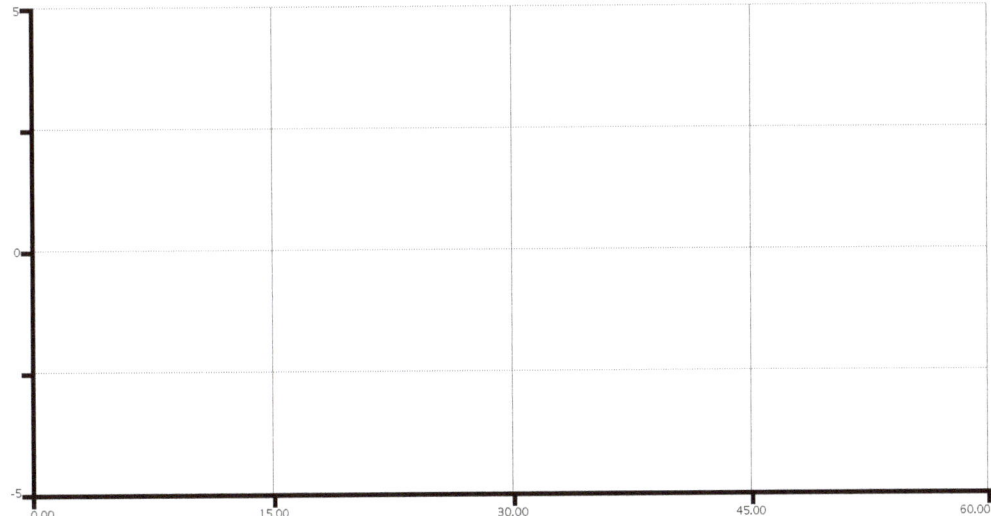

©2014 Creative Learning Exchange

Experimental Run (continued)

a. Explain why you think the spring changed as it did.

b. Approximately how much time does it take for the spring to go through one cycle?

c. What do you think is impacting the speed of the oscillation cycle?

d. How does this run compare to the baseline run?

e. What's similar?

f. What's different?

g. What is causing the similarities and differences?

LESSON 1, LEVEL C, HANDOUT 3 – P.1

Springs Everywhere – Debrief

Click Menu. **Click 3. Debrief Central.** You'll go through each of these debrief sections to think about what you experienced in the simulation.

Click A. Behavior Patterns. Read and then **click** Continue.
a. What two elements must be at '0' for the spring to be at rest?

b. Why?

Click Continue.
c. What effect does resistance produce on a spring?

d. What is the difference between high and low resistance?

Click Continue. **Click** Next Section. Back at the Menu, **click B. Explore the Model.**
Click and read through Tour the Model Structure and Tour the Loops. (**Click** on the arrow to go back to one from the other.)
a. Look at the map below and use it to answer the questions on the next page.

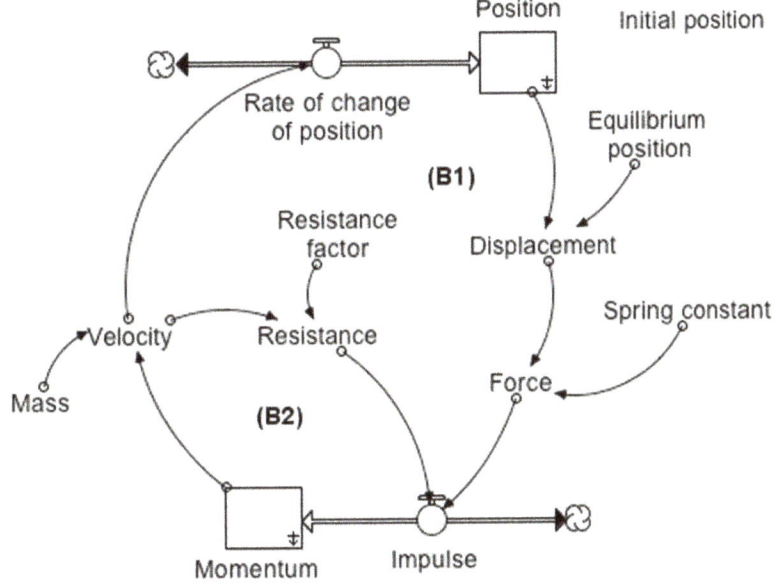

©2014 Creative Learning Exchange

LESSON 1, LEVEL C, HANDOUT 3 – P.2

Debrief (continued)

b. Explain the elements, connections, and loops within the map; (see previous page). *Hint*: follow the cause-and-effect arrows around, describing the connections along the way. The two loops are B1 (balancing loop 1), which causes the spring to oscillate up and down, and B2 (balancing loop 2), which causes the spring to slow and stop.

c. How did setting the initial position higher or lower affect the spring?

d. How did changing the spring constant affect the spring?

e. How did changing the mass affect the spring?

Click Next Section. Back at the Menu, **click C. Connections.**
a. How are springs and bungee cords similar and different in terms of their structure and behavior?

Debrief (continued)

b. Why do springs oscillate?

Click Continue.
c. What happens if you compress or stretch a spring?

Click Continue.
d. In your own words, explain what was done to make the Millennium Bridge safe to walk on.

e. What other systems oscillate in a similar way to a spring?

f. Why do they do this, specifically and in general?

LESSON 1, LEVEL C, HANDOUT 4 – P.1

Springs Everywhere – Assessment

a. What approximate settings would create the following graphs? You can fill in numerical values and/or qualifiers, such as high mass, low mass, no resistance, some resistance, etc.

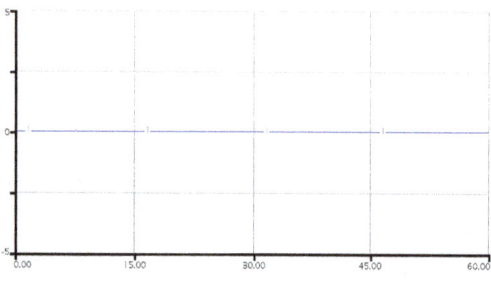

Change Position	
Mass	
Spring Constant	
Resistance	

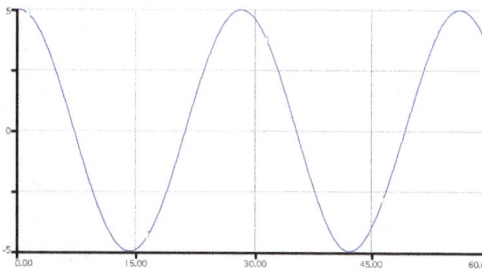

Change Position	
Mass	
Spring Constant	
Resistance	

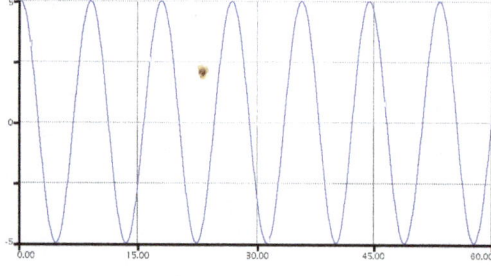

Change Position	
Mass	
Spring Constant	
Resistance	

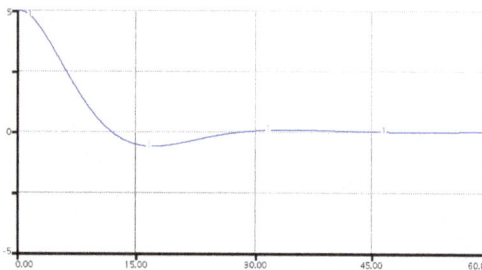

Change Position	
Mass	
Spring Constant	
Resistance	

b. How would you summarize your learning experience?

Final Run with Assessment of Graph Connections

Go back to Menu and to **2. Experiment with the Model**.
Set up the simulation as follows and then run the simulation.

Change Position	-5
Mass	2
Spring Constant	0.1
Resistance	0.1

You should get the following graphs. Notice the arrows showing the basic connections among these elements in the simulation. On a separate paper, define each element and tell the "story" of why they are connected in this way. For example, you can start with, "As the position of the spring rises toward 0 (see the line going up), the displacement goes down toward 0...."

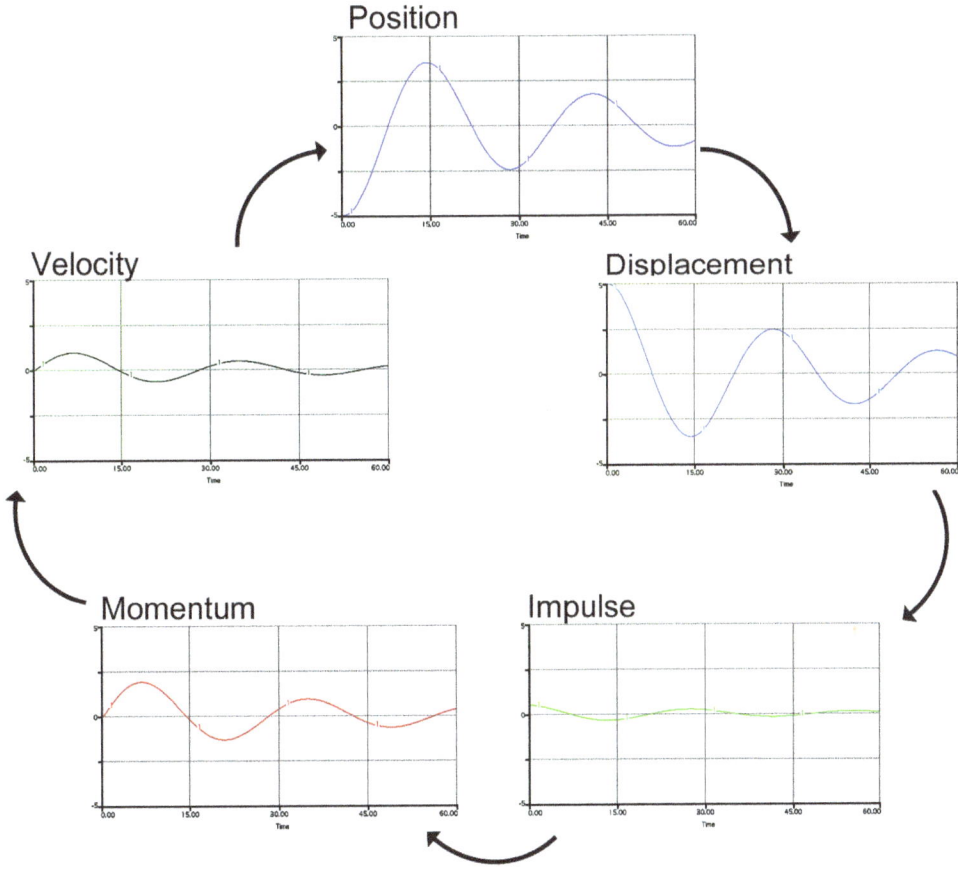

Lesson 2 – Level C

Romeo and Juliet: In Rapturous Oscillation?

Overview

This simulation allows students to explore relationship dynamics through the lens of Shakespeare's characters—Romeo and Juliet. Romeo and Juliet are put into a new context in which their feelings oscillate from love on one extreme to hate on the other. Students can change settings, run the simulation, and compare results. By changing the settings, a variety of behaviors are generated.

Learning Goals

- Represent, interpret, and compare data on a graph.
- Explain concepts including oscillation, contrarian, follower.
- Describe the system's interdependent relationships, connecting this particular oscillating structure to other types of relationships.

FIGURE 1: Title Screen

Student Challenge

Create a variety of simulated, oscillating relationships. Explain each relationship within the context of the simulation as well as within real world situations.

LESSON 2 – LEVEL C – AGES 13+

Time
Two or three 45-minute sessions

Materials
- One computer for every 2–3 students
- Handouts (See pages 35–46)

Curricular Connections
- "…examine contemporary patterns of human behavior…as they apply to individuals, societies and cultures."
- Analyze how complex characters (e.g., those with multiple or conflicting motivations) develop over the course of a text, interact with other characters….*

*Common Core State Standards

Key system dynamics concepts and insights
- Relationships between people (or entities) can produce behavior patterns such as oscillation between a leader (or contrarian) and a follower.
- A love-hate relationship between two people can be compared to a physical system such as a spring.

Additional information

Lesson Details

Preparation

1. Create groups of 2–3 students each.
2. Check computers to make sure you can access the online simulation.
3. Copy handouts for each student. See the chart below to determine how many copies of each handout you'll need.

#	Page	Handout	Description	Copies
1	35	Literature Connection (*Optional*)	If students have read Shakespeare's play, *The Tragedy of Romeo and Juliet*, they can graph the character dynamics throughout the story.	Copy single-sided. 1 copy per student
2	36–38	Introduction with Baseline Run	Students get started with the simulation using step-by-step directions.	Copy single-sided. 1 copy per student
			They then set up and record the data from a baseline run for Romeo and Juliet	Copy double-sided. 1 copy per student
3	39–40	Experimental Run	Students explore "What if?" questions, recording their data for each run. A minimum of three runs is recommended.	Copy double-sided. 3+ copies per student, depending on how many runs you'd like students to do.
4	41–43	Debrief	Students step through the debrief and write their reflections.	Copy double-sided. 1 copy per student
5	44–45	Assessment 1	Students summarize their learning.	Copy double-sided.
6	46	Assessment 2 (*Optional*)	Students synthesize the simulation results in order to make connections to other types of similar and different social relationships.	Copy single-sided.

4. *Optional*: You may want to read the background information about the underlying structure of the model. This can be useful as you guide students to understanding the model behavior, as it relates to real world behaviors, and the limitations of the model. (RomeoJuliet Model Background Info available as a separate file http://www.clexchange.org/ftp/documents/x-curricular/CC2012_Oscillations2BackgroundInformation.pdf)

Lesson Sequence

1. *Optional*: If students have read the play, *The Tragedy of Romeo and Juliet*, students can graph dynamics within the play using Handout 1. They can then compare those trends to the theoretical output of the simulation, which goes beyond the events of Shakespeare's play.

2. Introduce key vocabulary (e.g., contrarian, fickleness, follower, fatigue, oscillation) as needed.

3. Have students open the simulation and work through the simulation introduction and experiments, using the guided handouts. *Note that the handouts guide students through the simulation in a step-by-step manner. If you'd like to leave the exploration more open, then you may eliminate some of the handouts.* Figure 2 shows the control panel screen.

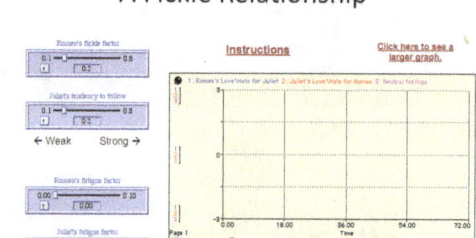

FIGURE 2: Control Panel

Debrief and Assessment

1. Have students use the debrief handouts to reflect on the simulation experience. You can also debrief the simulation experience as a class, using ideas for bringing the lesson home. Assessment 1 on pages 44–45 checks for basic understanding of concepts embedded within the simulation and allows students to make connections to other systems that exhibit similar trends. Assessment 2 on page 46 asks students to compare the simulated results with other real-world relationships.
2. See this and the following page for possible assessment responses.
   - Possible responses for questions 'a' and 'b' on Assessment 1, page 44:
     - **Question 'a'** – Example story of the graph: As Juliet's love for Romeo rises, Romeo, being fickle, starts losing interest. His love falls toward hatred. Juliet also loses interest because Romeo is no longer following. Now, Romeo realizes that Juliet is drifting away and reverses course, pursuing her in love once more. Juliet responds (as the follower) and loves him once again. Eventually, all the graphs reach neutrality, because they grow tired of the ups and downs. In the end, they are ambivalent toward one another.
     - **Question 'b'** – In order to create this graph, we'd need a low fickle factor, low tendency to follow, and some fatigue. The actual numbers used to produce the graph are also included in the table below.

Romeo's Fickle Factor	Low (0.3)
Juliet's Tendency to Follow	Low (0.3)
Romeo's Fatigue Factor	Some, but not too high (0.4)
Juliet's Fatigue Factor	Some, but not too high (0.4)

   - Possible responses for questions 'd' and 'e' on Assessment 1, page 45:
     - See Figure 3 for an example map based on transferring the Romeo and Juliet map to another context.
     - One possible "story" for the example map: My little sister and I love each other, but sometimes she drives me nuts. She's always following me around. When my sister wants to hang out with me, I get annoyed, so I don't really want to be around her. She notices and then goes away. When I see that she doesn't want to be with me anymore, I get worried that she really doesn't like me. So, I start asking her to hang out again. She does, and for a while, it's cool. Then she starts bugging me again, and the whole crazy thing repeats!

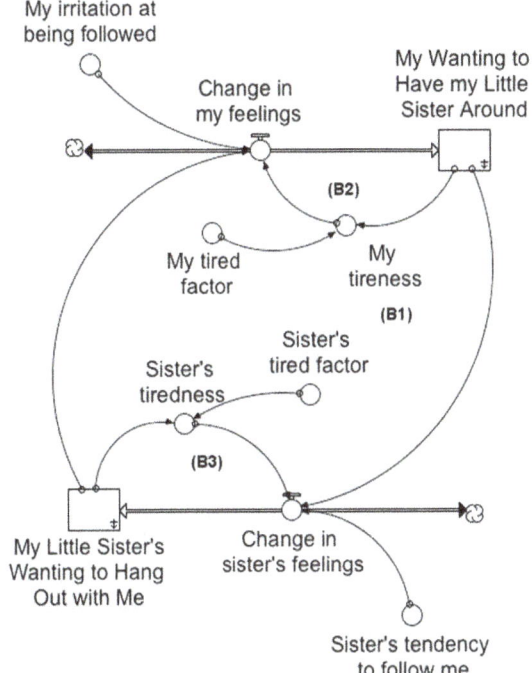

FIGURE 3: Example Map

Bringing the Lesson Home

- Discuss these and any other topics that have surfaced.
- What causes a relationship between two people (or entities) to oscillate? Come to a resting point?
- What caused faster oscillations? Slower?
- Analyze the simulation in terms of a tempestuous relationship between a man and a woman. Does the model make sense for that type of relationship? Why or why not?
- Literature connection: Discuss whether you agree or disagree with the following—Romeo and Juliet are kept apart, not by their families, but by "Romeo's fickleness."
- How does the simulation compare to other relationships, e.g., a feud or a conflict between two countries.

Assessment Ideas

Have students use the debrief and assessment handouts. The debrief takes students step-by-step through the debrief screens. The assessment allows students to create a connection to another situation.

ACKNOWLEDGEMENTS

Lesson 2 – Level C • Romeo and Juliet: In Rapturous Oscillation?
©2014 Creative Learning Exchange
www.clexchange.org

This model is one in a series of models that explores the characteristics of complex systems.

Model created with contributions from Jennifer Andersen, Anne LaVigne, Mike Radzicki, George Richardson, Lees Stuntz and with support from Jay Forrester and the Creative Learning Exchange.

Image Sources and Credits
The following images are in the public domain:
Title page from play - Source: http://commons.wikimedia.org/wiki/File:Romeoandjuliet1597.jpg
Romeo and Juliet painting - Source: http://commons.wikimedia.org/wiki/File:DickseeRomeoandJuliet.jpg
No love - Source: http://commons.wikimedia.org/wiki/File:No_love.svg
Mensa connections - Source: http://commons.wikimedia.org/wiki/File:Mensa_Connections.JPG; author Fitzftz
Reagan and Gorbachev - Source: http://commons.wikimedia.org/wiki/File:Reagan_and_Gorbachev_hold_discussions.jpg
Duck and Cover - Source: http://commons.wikimedia.org/wiki/File:Bert2.png
Graphic of nuclear stockpiles - Source: http://commons.wikimedia.org/wiki/File:US_and_USSR_nuclear_stockpiles.svg
The following images are used under the Creative Commons Attribution -Share Alike 3.0 Unported license (http://creativecommons.org/licenses/by-sa/3.0/deed.en) on either Wikipedia.org or Wikimedia Commons:
Red rose - Source: http://commons.wikimedia/wiki/File:Rosa_Red_Chateau01.jpg; author Hamachidori
Dried rose - Source: http://commons.wikimedia.org/wiki/File: DriedRose_063560.JPG; author Carolineee1991
Earth - Source: http://commons.wikimedia.org/wiki/File:Earths.jpg; author Stephen Slade Tien
Interlinking hearts - Source: http://commons.wikimedia.org/wiki/File:Love_Heart_symbol_rings.svg; author Nevit Dilmen
Planking - Source: http://commons.wikimedia.org/wiki/File:Planken.jpg; author J. de Vlaming
Silly Bands - Source: http://commons.wikimedia.org/wiki/File:Shaped_Rubber_Bands.JPG; author Stilfehler
The following image is used under the Creative Commons Attribution-Share Alike 2.5 Generic license (http://creativecommons.org/licenses/by-sa/2.5/deed.en) from Wikimedia Commons:
Internet sign - Source: http://commons.wikimedia.org/wiki/File:Internet-Sign.jpg; author cawi2001
The following image is used under the Creative Commons Attribution 2.0 Generic license (http://creativecommons.org/licenses/by/2.0/deed.en) from Wikimedia Commons:
Last petal - Source: http://commons.wikimedia.org/wiki/File:Last_petal_Loves_me.jpg; author Louise Docker (title page image)

LESSON 2, LEVEL C, HANDOUT 1 – P.1

Literature Connection to
The Tragedy of Romeo and Juliet

Choose two variables from the list below or create your own variables. Create at least two line graphs showing what happened over the course of the play, *Romeo and Juliet*.

Possible variables to graph:
- Romeo's Love for Juliet
- Juliet's Love for Romeo
- Level of Violence
- Animosity between Montegues and Capulets
- Other?

Describe your graph and justify using evidence from the text.

_____
_____
_____
_____
_____
_____
_____
_____
_____

I. II. III. IV. V.
Acts

Describe your graph and justify using evidence from the text.

_____
_____
_____
_____
_____
_____
_____
_____

I. II. III. IV. V.
Acts

©2014 Creative Learning Exchange

LESSON 2, LEVEL C, HANDOUT 2 – P.1

Romeo and Juliet –Introduction

Open web address: http://www.clexchange.org/curriculum/complexsystems/oscillation/
Select the "Romeo and Juliet: In Rapturous Oscillation? Level C simulation" and click, "Start."

You'll explore the sections (in **bold**) as indicated. Remember, you can always revisit a section anytime you like.

1. Click <u>Introduction – Love Dynamics</u>
a. Define the term "dyad" in your own words and give at least two examples.

b. What does it mean to be fickle in a relationship?

c. What does it mean to be a follower in a relationship?

Click <u>Menu</u>. Click <u>Experiment with the Model</u>. Click <u>Instructions</u>
Click on the "?" for each of the settings and then define these in your own words.
Romeo's Fickle Factor:

Juliet's Tendency to Follow:

Romeo's Fatigue Factor:

Juliet's Fatigue Factor:

Use the following worksheets to predict and record your virtual experiments.

Run # 1: Baseline Runs for Romeo and Juliet

Input the values shown below onto the simulation screen, but don't run it just yet.

Romeo's Fickle Factor	0.1
Juliet's Tendency to Follow	0.1
Romeo's Fatigue Factor	0
Juliet's Fatigue Factor	0

Predict: What do you think will happen to Romeo and Juliet's love for one another over time?

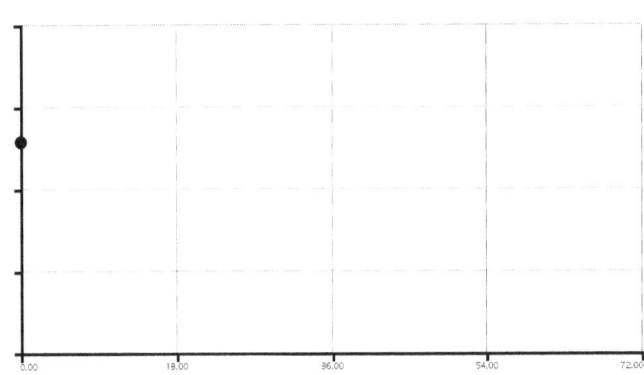

Draw and label your general prediction as two lines on the graph—one as Romeo's love/hate for Juliet and the other as Juliet's love/hate for Romeo. Note that they will both start at a level of 1, which is at the dot shown on the y-axis. Now **click "Run."**

Analysis: What actually happened? Using two colors, create a key, show the scale on the y-axis, and draw the graphs for Romeo and Juliet. Note that you can see the two graphs individually by clicking the tab at the bottom left corner of the graph.

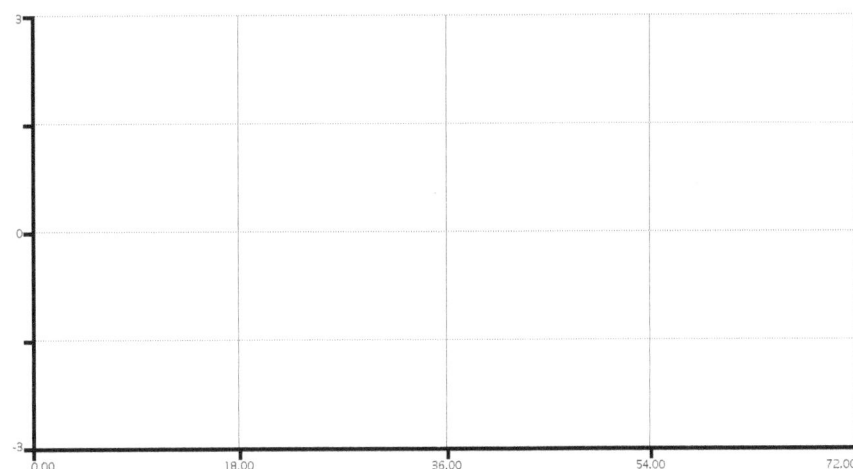

Baseline Run (continued)

a. Columnist Clarence Peterson speculated that Romeo and Juliet are kept apart in Shakespeare's play, not by their families, but by "Romeo's fickleness." If this were true, is this a good model of their relationship? Explain the trends on the graph in light of the concept of "Romeo's fickleness." Does "fickleness" explain the behavior you see?

b. Approximately how much time does it take for the relationship to go through one cycle? (*Hint:* Look at the time distance between two peaks for one of the lines on the graph. You can click and hold on a graph line to see the values.)

c. Why does the relationship appear to oscillate (go up and down) forever?

d. Given the graph on the previous page, what is your estimate as to the percent of time that both Romeo and Juliet are in love with one another "at the same time?" How could your prove your answer?

e. Continue your exploration, asking "What if" questions. Ask one question at a time and then record what happens on a new run sheet.

   Question 1: What might happen if Romeo was even more fickle and Juliet was even more of a follower?

   Question 2: What might happen if Juliet was more of a follower, but Romeo was less fickle?

   Question 3: What might happen if Romeo and Juliet became fatigued by "the game of ups and downs?"

   Question 4: What are some other questions you could explore? Write one or more questions below and try them one at a time.

LESSON 2, LEVEL C, HANDOUT 3 – P.1

Romeo and Juliet – Experimental Run

Run #: _____ **Question:** _____

Make sure to change only one setting from the baseline values that relates to your question.

Romeo's Fickle Factor	0.1
Juliet's Tendency to Follow	0.1
Romeo's Fatigue Factor	0
Juliet's Fatigue Factor	0

Predict: What do you think will happen to Romeo and Juliet's love for one another over time?

Draw and label your general prediction as two lines on the graph—one for Romeo's love/hate for Juliet and the other for Juliet's love/hate for Romeo. Note that they will both start at a level of 1, which is at the dot shown on the y-axis. Now **click "Run."**

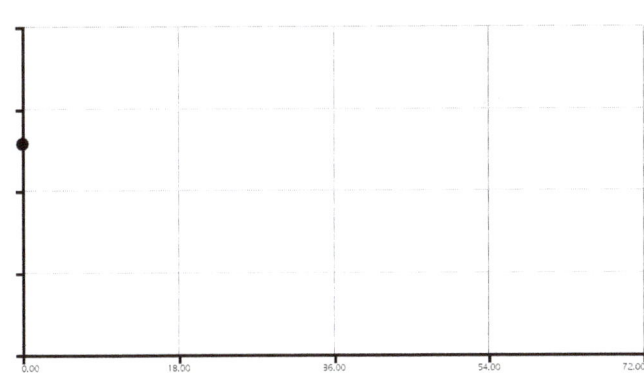

Analysis: What actually happened? Using two colors, create a key, show the scale on the y-axis, and draw the two lines.

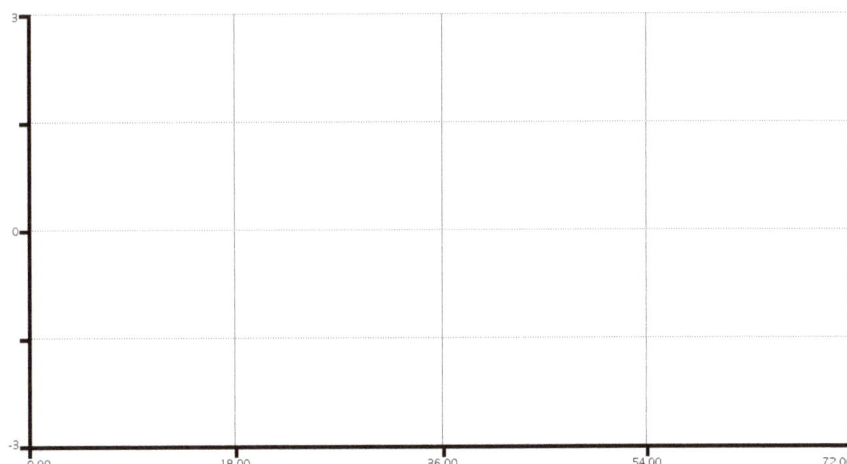

©2014 Creative Learning Exchange   LESSON 2 – Level C • Romeo and Juliet • 39

a. Explain why you think the relationship changed as it did.

b. Approximately how much time does it take for the relationship to go through one cycle?

c. What do you think is impacting the speed of the oscillation cycle?

d. How does this run compare to the baseline run?

e. What's similar?

f. What's different?

g. What is causing the similarities and differences?

LESSON 2, LEVEL C, HANDOUT 4 – P.1

Romeo and Juliet – Debrief

Click Menu. **Click 3. Debrief Central.** You'll go through each of these debrief sections to think about what you experienced in the simulation.

Click A. Behavior Patterns. Read and then **click** Explanation of the Graph.
a. Discuss Romeo's role as the contrarian in comparison to Juliet's role as the follower. Look up the term "contrarian" if needed.

Click Continue.
b. What causes faster vs. slower cycles within the relationship? Make sure to discuss specific settings that generate these behaviors.

Click Continue.
c. What causes the cycling to stop? Discuss in terms of the settings and how these are connected to real life examples.

Click Continue.
d. How do you explain this graph?

e. Who is most "stable" and who is the most "dramatic?" Why?

f. How do you think the fatigue factors are set in this run? How do you know?

©2014 Creative Learning Exchange

Click Next Section. Back at the Menu, **click B. Explore the Model.**
Click and read through Tour the Model Structure and Tour the Loops.
a. Look at the map below and use it to answer the questions on this and the next page.

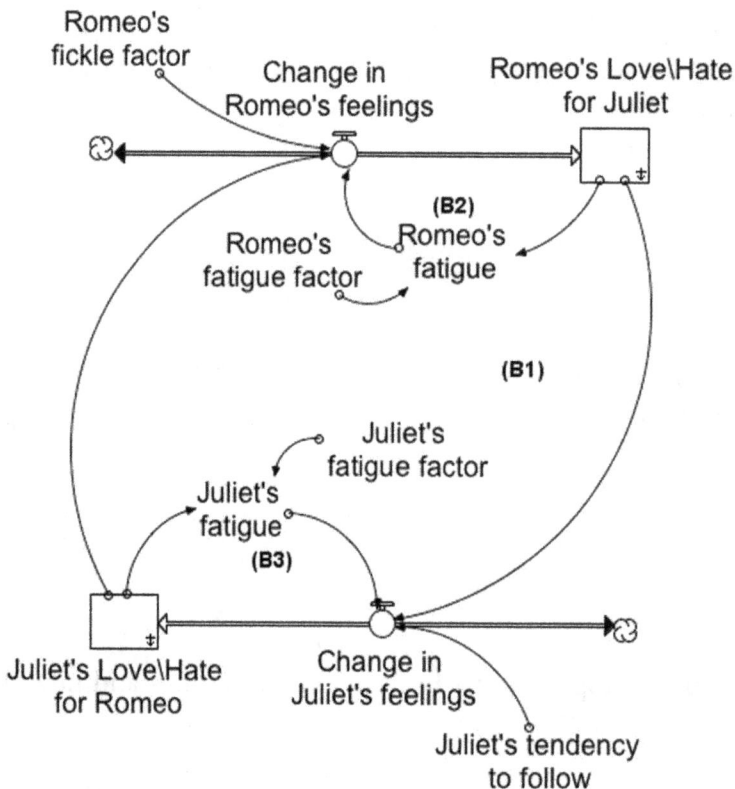

b. Explain the elements, connections, and loops within the map. *Hint:* follow the cause-and-effect arrows around describing the connections along the way. The three loops are B1 (balancing loop 1) which causes the relationship to oscillate up and down, B2 (balancing loop 2) which causes the relationship to stop cycling up and down, and B3 (balancing loop 3) which also causes the relationship to stop cycling up and down.

c. How did changing Juliet's tendency to follow affect the relationship over time?

d. How did changing Romeo's fickle factor affect the relationship over time?

e. How did changing either Romeo's or Juliet's fatigue factors affect the relationship over time?

Click Next Section. Back at the Menu, **click C. Connections.**
a. How are romantic relationships within the simulation and the interactions during the Cold War similar and different in terms of their structure and behavior over time?

Click Continue.
b. How are romantic relationships within the simulation and fads similar and different in terms of their structure and behavior over time?

c. What are other systems that oscillate in a similar way? Identify and describe at least two connections.

LESSON 2, LEVEL C, HANDOUT 5 – P.1

Romeo and Juliet – Assessment 1

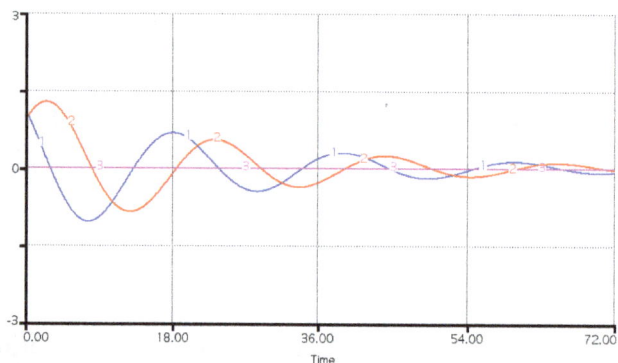

a. Tell the story of the lines on the graph. Why are they going up and down, and then stabilizing?

b. What approximate settings would create the graphs above? You can fill in numerical values and/or qualifiers, such as high fickle factor, low fickle factor, no fatigue, some fatigue, etc.

Romeo's Fickle Factor	
Juliet's Tendency to Follow	
Romeo's Fatigue Factor	
Juliet's Fatigue Factor	

c. How might the behaviors been different if the roles in the simulation were reversed, that is, if Juliet was fickle and Romeo was the follower?

LESSON 2, LEVEL C, HANDOUT 5 – P.2

d. Choose one of the connections you listed on the debrief handout or come up with another one. Using the map below, add labels to each of the elements to describe the interactions. You can use the map for Romeo and Juliet on Handout 4 to help you.

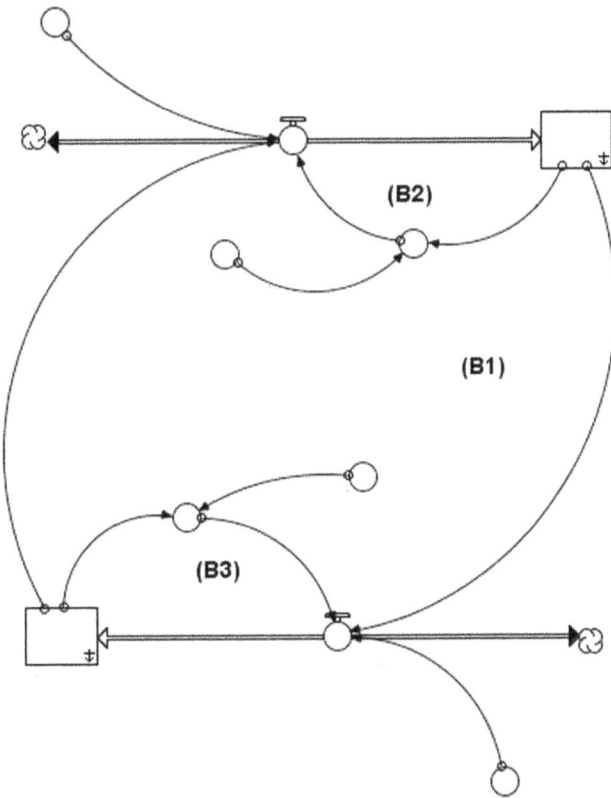

e. Tell the story of your map.

Romeo and Juliet – Assessment 2 (optional)

Think of a relationship in your own life or of two people from a book or story. For example, instead of a contrarian (Romeo) and a follower (Juliet), what if both people are enthusiastic about the relationship? What if one likes the other, but the feelings are never returned? How would love look between two shy, cautious people? What might feelings for a future spouse be, over the course of a long marriage? If a friendship was once strong but went cold over time, what would that look like?

Provide a short written description of the dynamics you see in this relationship. Who are the people involved—friends, relatives, fictional characters? There is no need to include identifying information if you're describing people from your own life. What happens in the relationship? Be sure to describe the time horizon: are the dynamics playing out over days, weeks or years? Try to describe the situation from both points of view.

On the graph below, sketch the relationship dynamics you've described. Using two colors, create a key, show the scale on the y-axis, and draw a line for each person's feelings of love and/or hate over time.

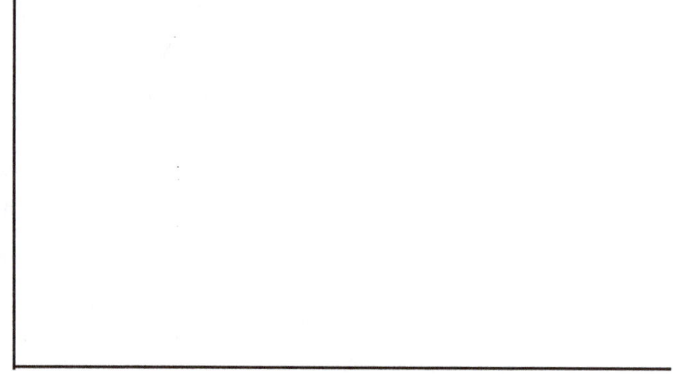

Finally, list some ideas for what might change the behavior of the relationship. If the relationship is positive, like friendship or love, what might cause it to sour, and vice versa?

Lesson 3 – Level C

Rabbits, Rabbits, and More Rabbits: Logistic Growth in Animal Populations

Overview

This simple population model explores a variety of animals limited only by their own population densities. Students can change various settings for each population, including birth factor, lifespan, and habitat area. Each of the populations does (or would eventually) level off as it reaches a carrying capacity.

Learning Goals

- Represent and interpret data on a line graph.
- Compare results for simulation runs.
- Explain the concept of density as pertaining to population dynamics.
- Represent a different animal on a map, including other factors that influence its growth or decline.

LESSON 3 – LEVEL C – AGES 13+

Time
Three or four 45-minute sessions

Materials
- One computer for every 2-3 students
- Handouts (See pages 51–60)

Curricular Connections
- Science: Populations, ecosystems, scientific method
- Math: Vary assumptions, explore consequences, and compare predictions with data.*

Common Core State Standards

Key system dynamics concepts and insights
- Populations may grow or decline to carrying capacity.
- Logistic growth is a combination of two processes—exponential growth in which animals can reproduce explosively because of an abundance of resources, followed by slowing of the growth due to limiting factors.

Additional information

FIGURE 1: Title Screen

Student Challenge

Compare animal populations in order to determine which population is most successful over time. Be able to explain why in terms of key concepts—population density and carrying capacity.

Lesson Details

Preparation

1. Create groups of 2–3 students each.
2. Check computers to make sure you can access the online simulation.
3. Copy handouts for each student. See the chart below to determine how many copies of each handout you'll need.

#	Page	Handout	Description	Copies
1	51	Introduction	Students get started with the simulation using step-by-step directions.	Copy single-sided. 1 copy per student
2	52–53	Experimental Run	Students explore "What if?" questions, recording their data for each run. A minimum of three runs is recommended.	Copy double-sided. 3+ copies per student, depending on how many runs you'd like students to do.
3	54	Comparison	Students compare animal populations on this summary page.	Copy single-sided. 1 copy per student
4	55–57	Debrief	Students step through the debrief and write their reflections.	Copy double-sided. 1 copy per student
5	58	Assessment 1	Students identify and describe connections between the simulation and other systems.	Copy single-sided. 1 copy per student
6	59–60	Assessment 2 and 3	Students choose one of these handouts to summarize their learning.	Copy single-sided. The number of copies needed of each depends on student choice.

4. *Optional:* You may want to read the background information about the underlying structure of the model. This can be useful as you guide students to understanding the model behavior, as it relates to real-world behaviors, and the limitations of the model. (Rabbits, Rabbits and More Rabbits Model Background Info available as a separate file http://www.clexchange.org/ftp/documents/x-curricular/CC2012_Oscillations3BackgroundInformation.pdf)

Lesson Sequence

1. Introduce students to any specific content knowledge related to ecosystems, animal populations, etc., that you would like students to have prior to running the simulation. This may include:
   - definitions of terms, such as, population, lifespan, area, population density, births factor (rate), deaths factor (rate), and carrying capacity.
   - degree of reproductive success, based on birth rate and lifespan.
2. Have students open the simulation and work through the simulation introduction, experiment, and debrief using the guided handouts. *Note that the handouts guide students through the simulation in a step-by-step manner. If you would like to leave the exploration more open, then you may eliminate some of the handouts.* Figure 2 shows the control panel screen.

Debrief and Assessment

1. Have students complete one or more assessment options. Assessment 1 focuses on the trends and connections. Assessments 2 and 3 are the same basic exercise, so students can select either one of them. Students can work independently or with a group to complete the diagrams. See Figures 3 and 4 for

example debrief responses. Note that these are only examples. Different representations are fine so long as students can justify their representation and they show an understanding of other elements that impact populations. By having students share their maps with the class or with another small group, they can further clarify their understanding. They may then choose to modify their own diagrams, based on seeing and hearing others' explanations. For this reason, completing the diagrams in pencil allows for this modification process to occur more easily.

2. Debrief the simulation experience as a class using ideas for bringing the lesson home.

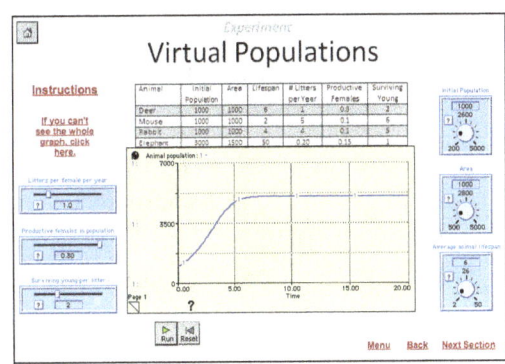

FIGURE 2: Control Panel

Bringing the Lesson Home

Discuss these and any other questions that have surfaced about model behaviors.

- What caused the populations to grow and then level off?
- As human population grows, what are possible consequences for large animal species that need a lot of space to live?
- For animals that reproduce slowly, what can happen when their populations drop to very low numbers? What does it mean for a population to be "viable" or "sustainable" over the long term?
- How do the dynamics in this simulation about animals compare to human population dynamics?

Assessment Ideas

- Assessment 1: Connect the simulation's trends to other similar systems.
- Assessments 2/3: Modify the original simulation map (or feedback loops). Then add new structures to show other elements that impact populations and "tell the story" of the map.

ACKNOWLEDGEMENTS

Lesson 3 – Level C • Rabbits, Rabbits, and More Rabbits: Population Dynamics: Logistic Growth
©2014 Creative Learning Exchange
www.clexchange.org

This model with accompanying lesson is one in a series that explores the characteristics of complex systems. Model created with contributions from Jen Andersen, Anne LaVigne, Michael Radzicki, George Richardson, Lees Stuntz, and with support from Jay Forrester and the Creative Learning Exchange.

Image Credits
The following images are in the public domain:
Mouse - Source: http://commons.wikimedia.org/wiki/File:Tiny_mouse_frozen_in_fear_in_the_Himalayas.jpg; author Madhur D'silva
Deer - Source: http://commons.wikimedia.org/wiki/File:White-tailed_deer.jpg; author Scott Bauer, USDA

Mensa connections - Source: http://commons.wikimedia.org/wiki/File:Mensa_Connections.JPG; author Fitzftz
Population density map - Source: http://commons.wikimedia.org/wiki/File:USA_2000_population_density.png; originally obtained from National Atlas of the United States, a work of the U.S. federal government
The following image is used under the Creative Commons Attribution-Share Alike 2.5 Generic license (http://creativecommons.org/licenses/by-sa/2.5/deed.en) on Wikimedia Commons:
Internet sign - Source: http://commons.wikimedia.org/wiki/File: Internet-Sign.jpg; author cawi2001
The following images are used under the Creative Commons Attribution-ShareAlike 3.0 Unported license (http://creativecommons.org/licenses/by-sa/3.0/deed.en) on either Wikipedia.org or Wikimedia Commons:
African elephant - Source: http://

commons.wikimedia.org/wiki/File:ElephantAfricanKenia.JPG; author Sumurai8
Rabbits on campus - Source: http://commons.wikimedia.org/wiki/File:UVic_rabbits.jpg; author Jeffery J. Nichols
US population graph - Source: http://commons.wikimedia.org/wiki/File:US_Population,_1790_-_2011.svg; authors Stephanie Hernandez and David Joerg, based on US Census Bureau and CIA World Factbook data
Fawn - Source: htt p://commons.wikimedia.org/wiki/File:Fawn-in-grass.jpg; author ForestWander
Earth - Source: http://commons.wikimedia.org/wiki/File:Earths.jpg; author Stephen Slade Tien

Notes about the example diagrams

- Additions to the map and causal loop diagrams are shown in blue.

- One possible "story" to accompany the loop diagram (Figure 3) is: As human development goes up, there's more DDT use and also less area for the condors to live in. Luckily, as the condor population drops, human concern rises and leads to conservation efforts, such as a decrease in DDT use and increases in captive breeding programs, which over time have helped the condor population to grow.

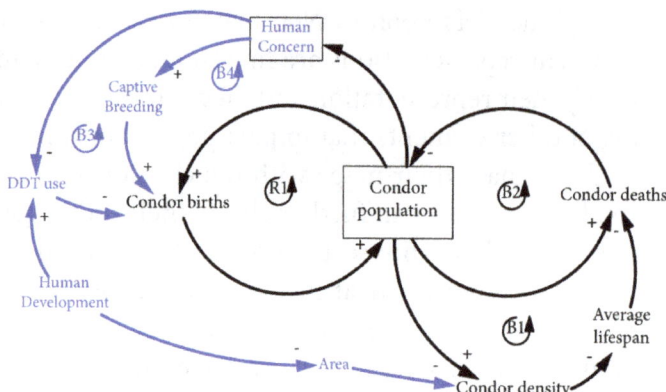

FIGURE 3: Example of Completed Loops for Assessment 3, page 14

- One possible "story" to accompany the stock/flow map (Figure 4) is: Human development and hunting have impacted the death flow of the condor population. Human development decreases the habitat (area) that is available to the condor population. To offset these negative impacts, people have started various programs and policies. DDT was outlawed and is no longer in use. Initiation of a captive breeding program increased the number of births over time.

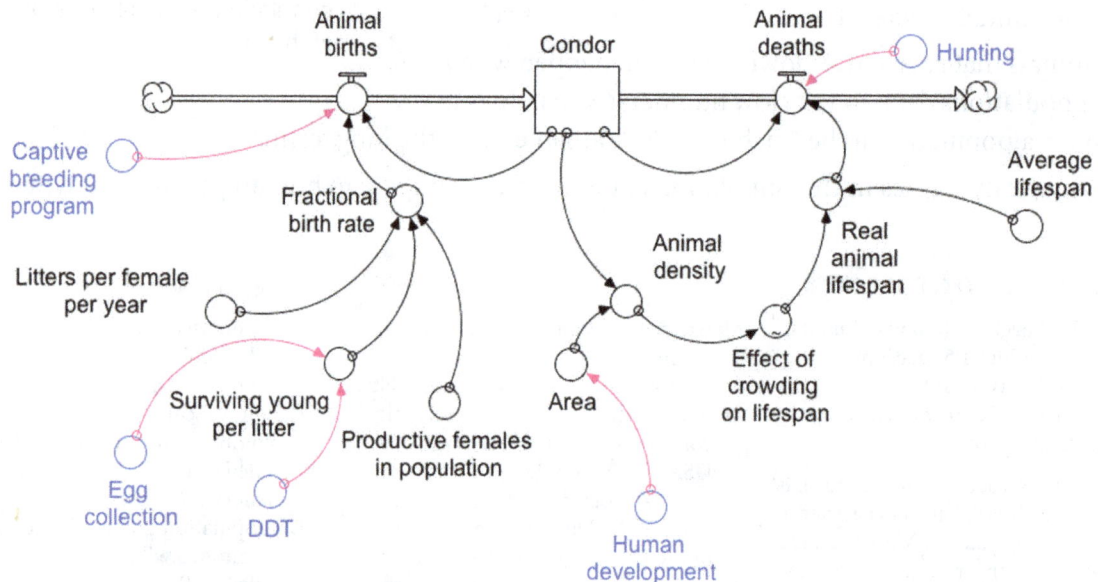

FIGURE 4: Example Completed Stock/Flow Map for Page 13 Assessment

LESSON 3, LEVEL C, HANDOUT 1 – P.1

Rabbits, Rabbits, and More Rabbits – Introduction

Open web address: http://www.clexchange.org/curriculum/complexsystems/oscillation/
Select the "Rabbits, Rabbits, and More Rabbits: Logistic Growth in Animal Populations-Level C simulation" and **click**, "Start."

You'll explore the sections (in **bold**) as indicated. Remember, you can always revisit a section anytime you like.

1. Click Introduction – Population Dynamics.
a. What are some elements that affect the growth and decline of populations?

b. Describe and give examples of density-dependent and density-independent factors that limit populations.

Click Continue.
c. What is logistic growth?

d. Why did the microbe population in the petri dishes stop growing?

Click Menu.
2. Click Experiment with the Model.
You will use the following worksheets to predict and record your virtual experiments.

LESSON 3, LEVEL C, HANDOUT 2 – P.1

Rabbits, Rabbits, and More Rabbits – Simulation Record Sheet

Simulation Record Sheet for Animal: _____

Initial population	
Productive females in population	
Litters per female per year	
Surviving young per litter	
Average animal lifespan	
Area	
Final Population	

Predict: What do you think will happen to the population?

Draw your general prediction as a line on the graph. Note that the dot shows an initial population of 1000 animals. Now **click** "Run."

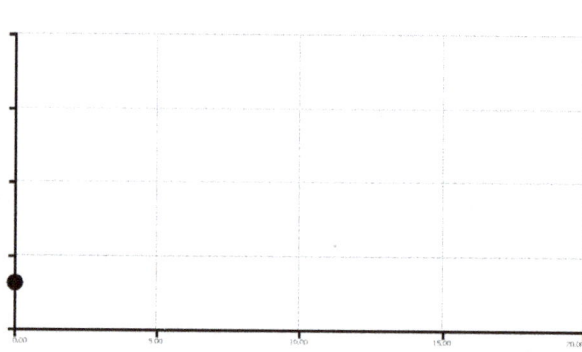

Analysis: What actually happened?
a. Record the final population numbers in the table at the top of the page.
b. Title the graph, create a key, show the scale on the y-axis, and draw the graph for the population. Label the line "Run 1."

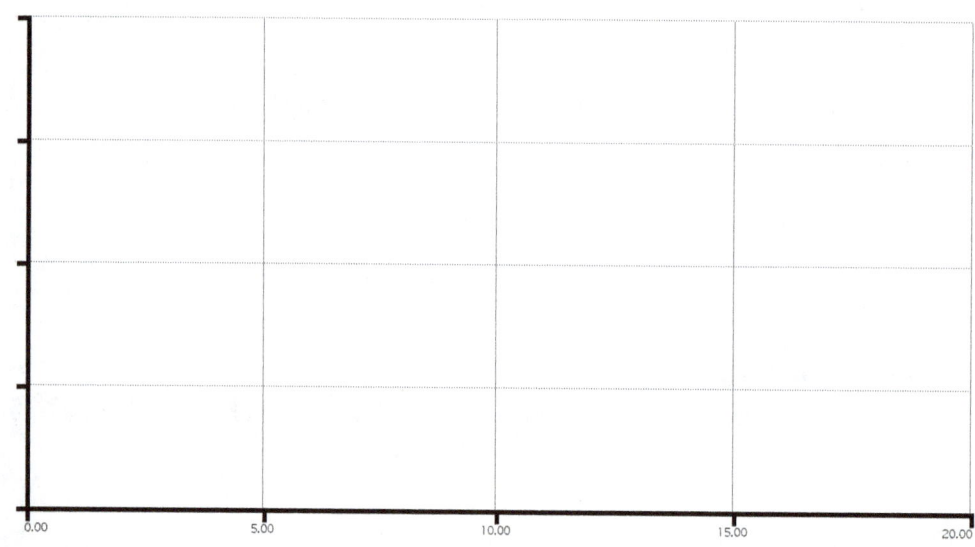

c. What happened to the population over time? Why?

d. Repeat the simulation, changing just one element.
   What element would you like to change?: _____
   Setting: _____

Predict: What do you think will happen to the population?

Draw your general prediction as a line on the graph. Note that the dot shows an initial population of 1000 animals. Now **click** "Run."

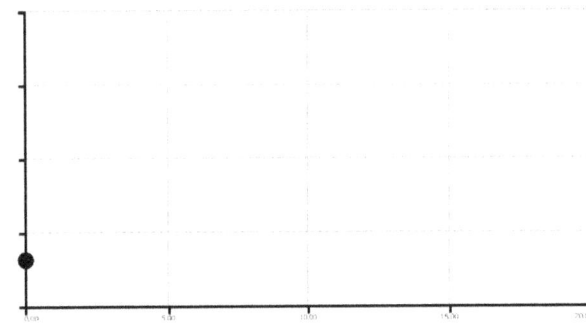

Draw a new line on the graph on the previous page, labeling it, "Run 2."
Look at both graphs.

e. How are the two trend lines similar?

f. How are the two trend lines different?

g. What is causing both the similarities and differences?

LESSON 3, LEVEL C, HANDOUT 3 – P.1

Rabbits, Rabbits, and More Rabbits – Animal Comparisons

Create a key for each of the animals and draw the trends on the graph below. Record only the first run for each animal.

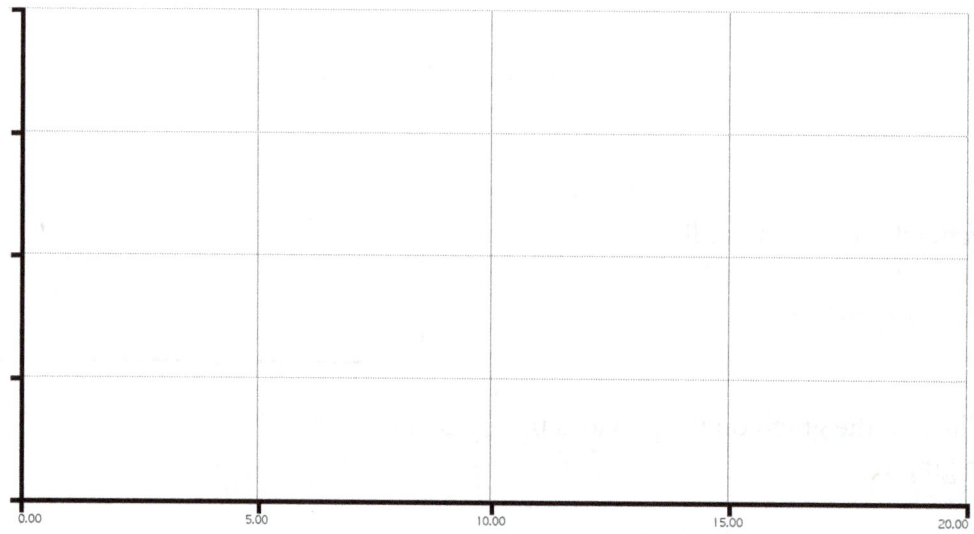

a. How are the trends similar and different?

b. Using vocabulary from the simulation, explain why the population dynamics are similar.

c. Which population grew most quickly? Why?

d. Which population grew most slowly? Why?

LESSON 3, LEVEL C, HANDOUT 4 – P.1

Rabbits, Rabbits, and More Rabbits – Debrief

Click Menu.
Click Debrief Central. You'll go through each of the sections of the debrief to process what you experienced in the simulation.

Click A. Behavior Patterns.
Read, look at the graphs, and **click** on "Carrying Capacity." Then answer the following:
a. Compare the graphs. What explains the differences for the three populations shown?

b. What is your hypothesis as to why large animal species, such as tigers, elephants, bears, and wolves are in decline?

c. In your own words, what is "carrying capacity?"

d. With human population at 7 billion and growing, how can we ensure the survival of other species?

e. What role might technology play, both in saving and destroying other species (and our own species)?

Click Continue.
f. What explains the behavior on this graph?

Click Continue.

g. Why did the sheep grow, then level off, while the lynx and hare show a clear oscillation over time?

h. Why does this simulation show only logistic growth, like the graph on the left, and not oscillation, like the graph on the right?

Click Continue. Read and **click**, Explanation of the graph.

i. Notice that the red line shows the net births. Net births are equal to the births minus the deaths. The blue line shows how many animals there are all together. Explain why the population continues to grow while the net births go down.

Click Menu and then **B. Explore the Model**. **Click**, Tour the Model Structure. Then answer the following:

a. What does the term "Density Dependent" mean?

b. How does crowding affect lifespan in the simulation? Why?

Click Tour the Loops. **Click** on the B (Balancing) and R (Reinforcing) symbols for the explanations.

c. In your own words, what is "reinforcing feedback?"

d. List two other examples of reinforcing feedback.

e. In your own words, what is "balancing feedback?"

f. List two other examples of balancing feedback.

Click Menu and then **C. Connections**.
a. When you look at this graph, do you think the United States has reached its carrying capacity for human beings? Why or why not?

b. How many more people do you think could be added, or how many fewer should there be?

Click Continue. Read, **click** Continue, and then answer the following:
c. If you had to guess, where would it be cheapest to buy land to build a house? Why?

d. Where would jobs be most plentiful? Why do you think this could be the case?

LESSON 3, LEVEL C, HANDOUT 5 – P.1

Rabbits, Rabbits, and More Rabbits – Assessment 1

a. Look at the graph, which is similar to many of the animal populations that grew and reached a carrying capacity.

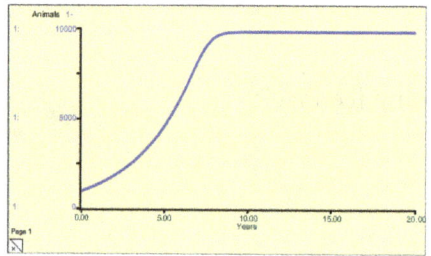

b. What elements were missing from this simulation that would give a more accurate picture of what impacts animal populations in the wild?

c. What other situations in the world would create a similar trend, that is, it grows for awhile, but then levels off over time? Make a quick list of as many examples as you can.

d. Choose one of your ideas and tell the story of the graph above, using the example you identified.

LESSON 3, LEVEL C, HANDOUT 6 – P.1

Rabbits, Rabbits, and More Rabbits – Assessment 2

a. Choose one of the animals from the simulation (or another one you researched) and refine the labels on the map for that animal.

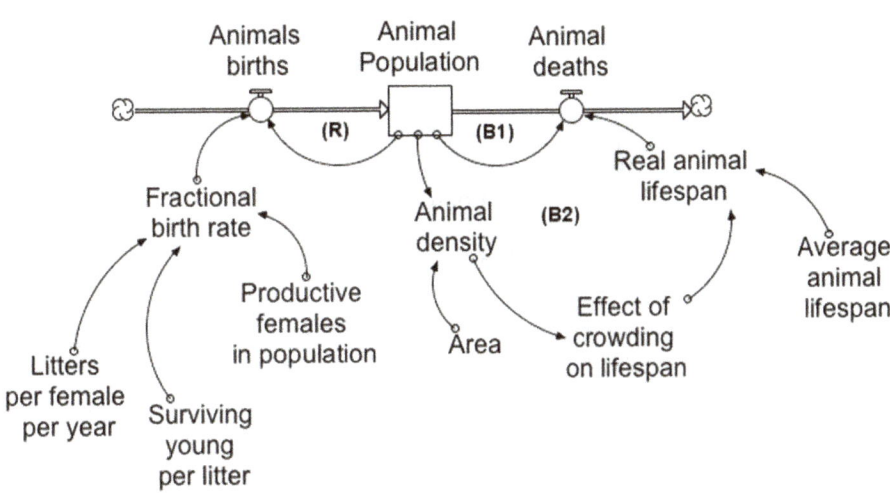

b. What elements would you need to add to the map to make it more realistic? Add at least two other elements along with related causal connections to the diagram above.

c. In summary, what story does the map tell about population growth and decline?

LESSON 3, LEVEL C, HANDOUT 6 – P.2

Rabbits, Rabbits, and More Rabbits – Assessment 3

a. Choose one of the animals from the simulation (or another one you researched) and refine the labels on the loop diagram for that animal.

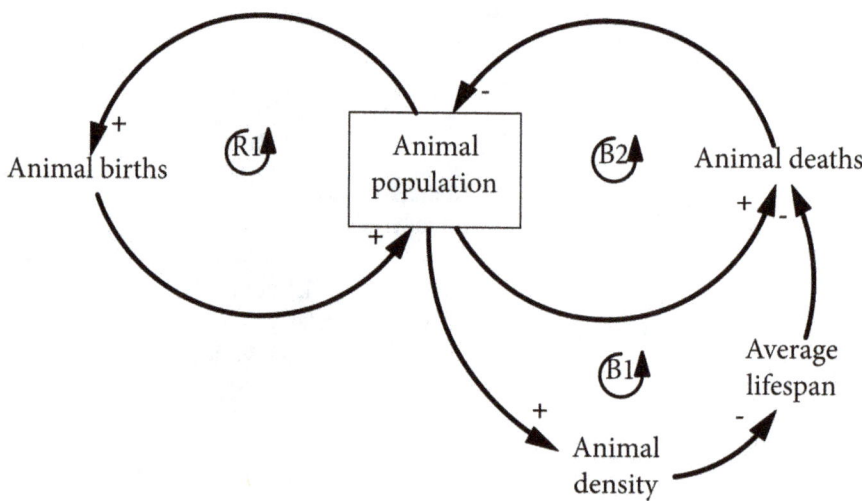

b. What elements would you need to add to the loop diagram to make it more realistic? Add at least two other elements along with related causal connections to the diagram above.

c. In summary, what story do the loops tell about population growth and decline?

Lesson 4 – Level C

Waves of Change: Predator and Prey Dynamics

Overview

The predator/prey model explores a moose and wolf population living on a small island. Students can change various components of a predator/prey model, including birth factor, lifespan, and habitat area. The default simulation behavior is oscillation of both prey and predator populations, in which the state of each population impacts the state of the other over time.

Learning Goals

- Represent and interpret data on a line graph.
- Compare results for simulation runs.
- Explain the concept of density with regard to population dynamics.
- Represent a food source for the moose on the simulation map or loop diagram.

LESSON 4 – LEVEL C – AGES 13+

Time
Three to four 45-minute sessions

Materials
- One computer for every 2–3 students
- Handouts (See pages 66–76)

Curricular Connections
- Science: Populations, ecosystems, scientific method
- Math: Vary assumptions, explore consequences, and compare predictions with data.*
- Reading: Analyze a complex set of ideas or sequence of events and explain how specific individuals, ideas, or events interact and develop over the course of the text.*

Common Core State Standards

Key system dynamics concepts and insights
- Individual populations do not exist in isolation, but rather interact over time.
- Predators and their prey form a type of complex system that can exhibit oscillatory behavior.

Additional information

FIGURE 1: Title Screen

Student Challenge

Given an analysis of what is causing the two populations to oscillate, create conditions which best stabilize (minimize the oscillations of) the ecosystem on the island.

©2014 Creative Learning Exchange

Lesson Details

Preparation

1. Create groups of 2–3 students each.
2. Check computers to make sure you can access the online simulation.
3. Copy handouts for each student. See the chart below to determine how many copies of each handout you'll need.

#	Page	Handout	Description	Copies
1	66–68	Introduction with Baseline Run	Students get started with the simulation using step-by-step directions. They then set up and record the data from a baseline run for the moose and wolves living on an island.	Copy single-sided. 1 copy per student Copy double-sided. 1 copy per student
2	69–70	Experimental Run	Students explore "What if?" questions, recording their data for each run. A minimum of three runs is recommended.	Copy double-sided. 3+ copies per student, depending on how many runs you'd like students to do.
3	71–72	Debrief	Students step through the debrief and write their reflections.	Copy double-sided. 1 copy per student
4	73–74	Final Run	Students work to complete a specific challenge.	Copy double-sided. 1 copy per student
5	75	Assessment 1	Students choose either this handout or handout #6 to summarize their learning.	Copy single-sided. The number of copies needed depends on student choice.
6	76	Assessment 2	Students choose either this handout or handout #5 to summarize their learning.	Copy single-sided. The number of copies needed depends on student choice.

4. *Optional:* You may want to read the background information about the underlying structure of the model. This can be useful as you guide students to understanding the model behavior, as it relates to real-world behaviors, and the limitations of the model. (Predator-Prey Model Background Info available as a separate file http://www.clexchange.org/ftp/documents/x-curricular/CC2012_Oscillations4BackgroundInformation.pdf)

Lesson Sequence

1. Introduce students to any specific content knowledge related to ecosystems, animal populations, etc., that you'd like students to have prior to running the simulation. This may include:
   - definitions of terms, such as, population, lifespan, area, population density, births factor (rate), deaths factor (rate), predator, and prey.
   - physical characteristics of predator and prey animals.
   - degree of specialization of predators in regard to food sources. In the initial case study of the moose/wolf populations, the wolf has a specialized diet, since moose is the main prey animal available within the island ecosystem.

2. Have students open the simulation and work through the simulation introduction, experiments, and debrief using the guided handouts. Note that the handouts guide students through the simulation in a step-by-step manner. If you'd like to leave the exploration more open, then you may wish to eliminate some of the handouts. Figure 2 shows the control panel screen.

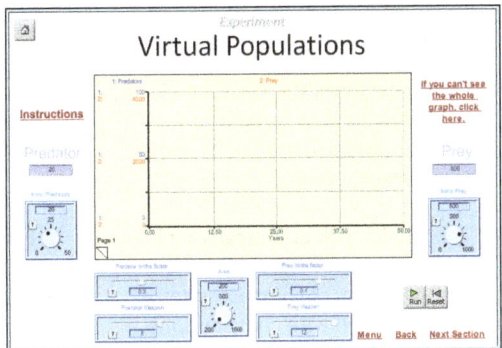

FIGURE 2: Control Panel

Debrief and Assessment

1. Have students select one of the assessments. Students can work independently or with a group to complete the diagrams. See Figures 3 and 4 for example debrief responses. Note that these are only examples of how students might represent a food source for the moose. Different representations are fine so long as students can justify their representation and they show an understanding of how moose and their food supply would impact one another. By having students share their maps with the class or with another small group, they can further clarify their understanding. They may then choose to modify their own diagrams, based on seeing and hearing others' explanations. For this reason, completing the diagrams in pencil allows for this modification process to occur more easily.

2. Debrief the simulation experience as a class using ideas for bringing the lesson home.

Assessment Ideas

Have students use one or more of the assessment handouts.

Assessments 1 and 2 allow students to take the original simulation map (or feedback loops) with moose and wolves shown explicitly. They then add new structure to show how the moose population needs a food source to survive. hey then 'tell the story' of the map, explaining how the structure produces oscillatory behavior.

Bringing the Lesson Home

Discuss these and any other questions that have surfaced about model behaviors.

- What caused the populations to oscillate?
- Why are the oscillations not exactly in sync with one another?
- What caused faster oscillations? Slower? Highest? Lowest?
- What settings created the most stable population numbers over time?
- How does the prey density affect both the prey and the predators?

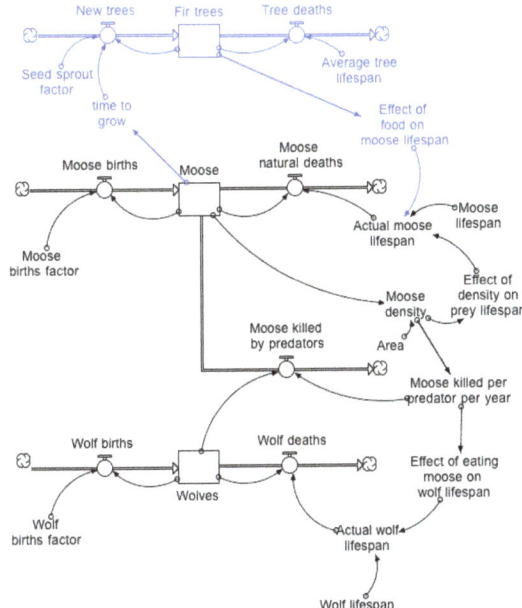

FIGURE 3: Example Completed Stock/Flow Map for Page 14 Assessment

©2014 Creative Learning Exchange

ACKNOWLEDGEMENTS

Lesson 4 – Level C • Waves of Change: Predator and Prey Dynamics
©2014 Creative Learning Exchange
www.clexchange.org

This model with accompanying lesson is one in a series that explores the characteristics of complex systems. Model created with contributions from Jen Andersen, Anne LaVigne, Michael Radzicki, George Richardson, Lees Stuntz, and with support from Jay Forrester and the Creative Learning Exchange.

Image Credits

The following images are in the public domain:

Wolf - Source: http://earthjustice.org/features/campaigns/wolf-recovery-under-attack-in-the-northern-rockies; author Gary Kramer, US Fish and Wildlife Service

Moose - Source: http://www.northshorenature.org/exhibits/mammals.php?pageNum_recordsCritters=2&totalRows_recordsCritters=5; US Fish and Wildlife Service

Hare - Source: http://en.wikipedia.org/wiki/File:Snowshoe_hare.jpg; Forest Service, US Department of Agriculture

Mink - Source: http://commons.wikimedia.org/wiki/File:AmericanMink.jpg; author National Park Service

Mensa connections - Source: http://commons.wikimedia.org/wiki/File:Mensa_Connections.JPG; author Fitzftz

The following images are used under the Creative Commons Attribution-ShareAlike 3.0 Unported license (http://creativecommons.org/licenses/by-sa/3.0/deed.en) on either Wikipedia.org or Wikimedia Commons:

Lynx - Source: http://commons.wikimedia.org/wiki/File:Canada_lynx_by_Michael_Zahra.jpg; author Michael Zahra

Muskrat - Source: http://commons.wikimedia.org/wiki/File:Musquash_hg.jpg; author Hannes Grobe

Deer crossing sign - Source: http://commons.wikimedia.org/wiki/File:DeerCrossingSign-crop.jpg; author SriMesh

Earth - Source: http://commons.wikimedia.org/wiki/File:Earths.jpg; author Stephen Slade Tien

US population graph - Source: http://commons.wikimedia.org/wiki/File:US_Population,_1790_-_2011.svg; authors Stephanie Hernandez and David Joerg, based on US Census Bureau and CIA World Factbook data

The following image is used under the Creative Commons Attribution-Share Alike 2.5 Generic license (http://creativecommons.org/licenses/by-sa/2.5/deed.en) on Wikimedia Commons:

Internet sign - Source: http://commons.wikimedia.org/wiki/File:Internet-Sign.jpg; author cawi2001

The following image is used under the Creative Commons Attribution-Share Alike 2.0 Generic license (http://creativecommons.org/licenses/by-sa/2.0/deed.en) on Wikimedia Commons:

A note about the example diagrams

(Additions to the map and causal loop diagrams are shown in blue.)

One possible "story" to accompany the map and loop diagrams is:
As the number of fir trees increase, the moose will have more available food, creating an effect of food on lifespan. As the lifespan increases, the moose population will increase due to fewer deaths. The larger moose population will eat more of the new tree growth, thus increasing how long it takes for the trees to grow. If they eat too much, over time, the tree population could decline. Now the moose will have less food, which could decrease their lifespan.

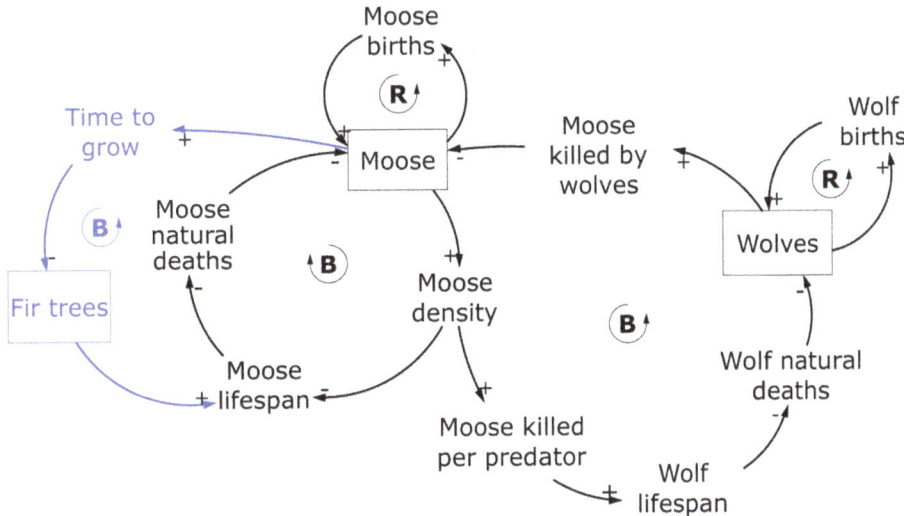

FIGURE 4: Example Completed Loops for Page 76 Assessment

Predator and Prey Dynamics – Introduction

Open web address: http://www.clexchange.org/curriculum/complexsystems/oscillation/
Select the "Waves of Change: Predator and Prey Dynamics – Level C simulation" and **click** "Start."

You'll explore the sections (in **bold**) as indicated. Remember, you can always revisit a section anytime you like.

1. Click <u>Introduction – Population Dynamics</u>.
a. When does logistic growth generally occur?

b. Give an example of this type of situation.

c. What shape would logistic growth produce on a line graph?

Click <u>Continue</u>.
Read "Predator-Prey Cycles." Look closely at the two graphs.
a. What patterns do you see in the Moose & Wolves graph on the right? How do the two populations seem to respond to each other over time?

b. What patterns do you see in the Hares & Lynx graph down on the left? How do the two populations seem to respond to each other over time?

Click <u>Menu</u>.
2. Click <u>Experiment with the Model</u>.
You will use the following worksheets to predict and record your virtual experiments.

Run # 1: Baseline Run for Wolves and Moose on Isle Royale

Click on the **?** for each of the sliders and dials to see what each one does. Input the values shown below onto the simulation screen, but don't run it just yet.

Predator	Wolf
Initial predators	20
Births factor	0.3
Normal lifespan	8 years
Area	200 square miles
Final # of Predators	

Prey	Moose
Initial prey	800
Births factor	0.4
Normal lifespan	12 years
Final # of Prey	

Predict: What do you think will happen to the two populations?

Draw your general prediction as lines on the graph, showing both the predator and prey populations in two different colors. Now **click** "Run."

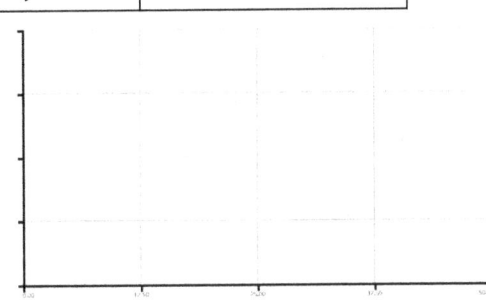

Analysis: What actually happened?
a. Record the final population numbers in the table at the top of the page.
b. Using two colors, create a key, show the scales on the y-axis, and draw the graphs for the two populations.

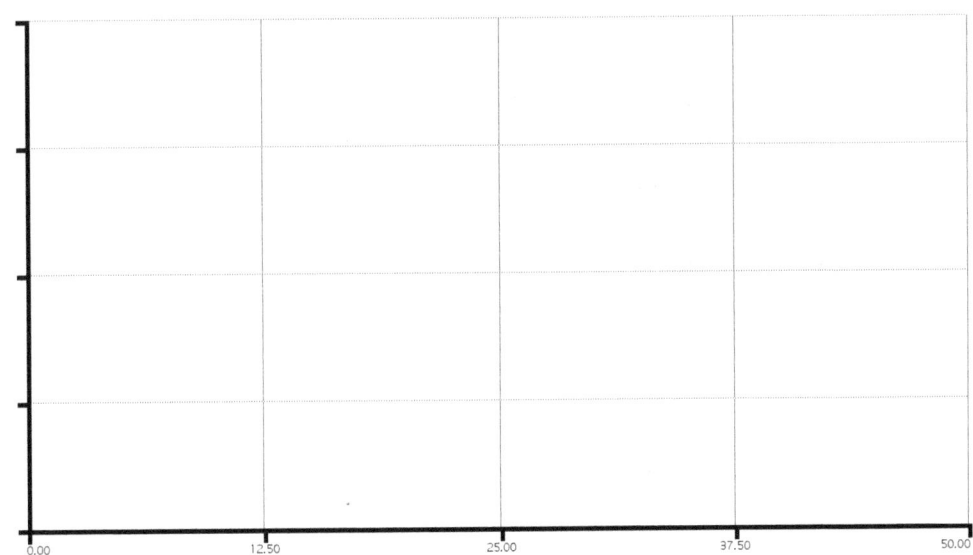

c. Explain why the populations changed as they did. Make sure to discuss how and why the populations impacted one another. *Optional:* Include a visual representation of the relationships between the predator and prey populations.

d. Approximately how much time does it take for the prey to go through one cycle? (*Hint:* On the graph, look at the time distance between two peaks. You can click and hold on the graph line to see the values.)

e. What do you think is impacting the speed of the oscillation cycle?

f. Continue your exploration, asking "What if" questions. Ask one question at a time and then record what happens on a new run sheet.

Question 1: What might happen if the animals had <u>less space</u> to live?

Question 2: What might happen if the animals had <u>more space</u> to live?

Question 3: What might happen if the island had <u>more wolves</u> to start?

Question 4: What might happen if the island had <u>fewer moose</u> to start?

Question 7: What are some other questions you could explore? Write one or more questions below and try them one at a time.

LESSON 4, LEVEL C, HANDOUT 2 – P.1

Predator and Prey Dynamics – Experimental Run

Run #: _____ **Question:** _____

Make sure to change only the one setting from the baseline values that relates to the question.

Predator	Wolf		Prey	Moose
Initial predators			Initial prey	
Births factor			Births factor	
Normal lifespan			Normal lifespan	
Area				
Final # of Predators			Final # of Prey	

Predict: What do you think will happen to the two populations based on this change?

Draw your general prediction as lines on the graph, showing both the predator and prey populations in two different colors. Now **click** "Run."

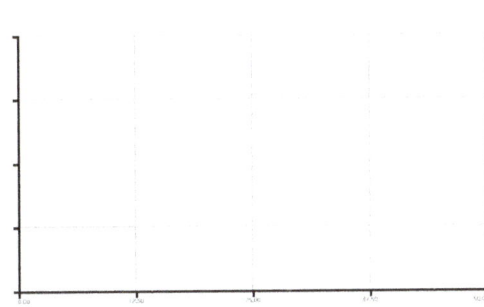

Analysis: What actually happened?
a. Record the final population numbers in the table above.
b. Using two colors, create a key, show the scales on the y-axis, and draw the graphs for the two populations.

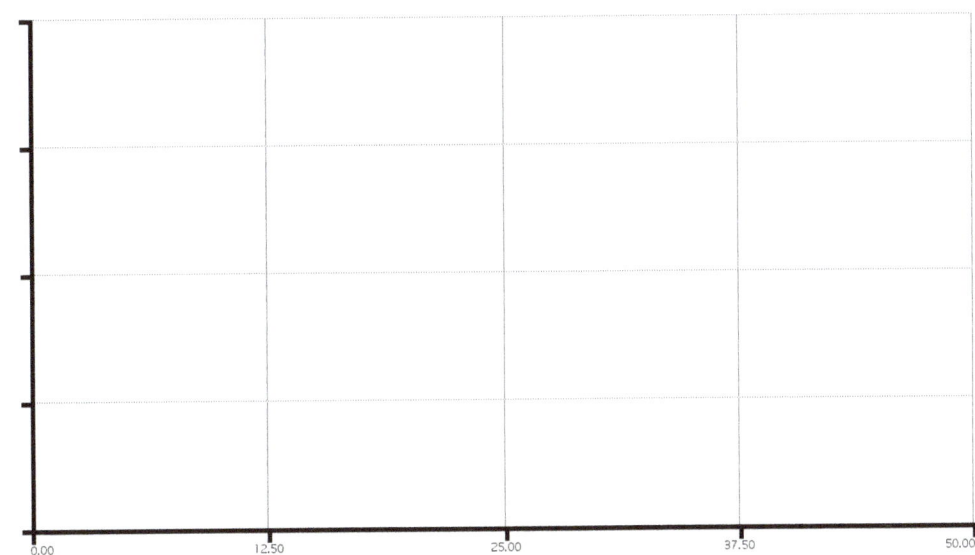

c. Explain why you think the populations changed as they did. Make sure to discuss how and why the populations impacted one another. *Optional:* Include a visual representation of the relationships between the predator and prey populations.

d. Approximately how much time does it take for the prey to go through one cycle?

e. What do you think is impacting the speed of the oscillation cycle?

f. How does this run compare to the baseline run?

What's similar?

What's different?

What is causing the similarities and differences?

LESSON 4, LEVEL C, HANDOUT 3 – P.1

Predator and Prey Dynamics – Debrief

Click Menu.
Click **Debrief Central.** You'll go through each of these sections of the debrief to process what you experienced in the simulation.

Click **A. Behavior Patterns.**
Read 1–4 and follow the steps through the Stock-Flow Diagram.
a. Answer the new question #1. Now there are fewer prey animals. What happens next?

Click results in this behavior. Read and evaluate your answer above. Change if necessary.

Go Back and then Continue. Read "No Cycles?" and look carefully at the graph. Answer the following:
a. What is carrying capacity? (Use a Biology text or Internet source.)

b. What settings might have caused the predators to die off and the prey in this graph to stabilize?

Click Explanation of the graph. Read carefully and evaluate your answer above.
Modify your answer above if necessary.

Close the explanation box and **Click** Continue.

Read "Population Density" and look carefully at the values in the T-chart and the graph.
Answer the following:
a. What is prey density?

b. What is the saturation point for prey density in this graph?

Click Next Section.
Back at the Menu, **click B. Explore the Model.**
Read "Model as Hypothesis" and answer the following:

a. Explain why high density of hares is good for the lynx but bad for the hares.

b. What's your best guess as to why the lynx don't just find something else to eat when the rabbit population density is low?

Click Tour the Model Structure. Use the space bar to see one piece added at a time.

a. In your own words, explain why these relationships among predator and prey cause the populations to oscillate (go up and down) over time.

Click Tour the Loops. **Click** on the B (Balancing) and R (Reinforcing) symbols for the explanations.

a. Decide which type of diagram you like and pick up the handout with that diagram, either Assessment 1 or Assessment 2.

b. Add to the diagram, given the moose's need for a food source.

Back at the Menu, **click C. Connections.**

a. Read through the three screens on Connections. Then list and describe one or more examples in the world that behave in a similar way to the predator and prey populations, cycling up and down over time.

Predator and Prey Dynamics – Final Run Question

What settings produce the most stable populations (with low, slow oscillations) over time?

You can complete multiple runs before recording your best run on this sheet. When making changes, consider whether you have (as a human) control over that change. For example, you would not be able to have a huge impact on the birth factor or lifespan.

Predator	Wolf
Initial predators	
Births factor	
Normal lifespan	
Area	
Final # of Predators	

Prey	Moose
Initial prey	
Births factor	
Normal lifespan	
Final # of Prey	

Analysis: What actually happened?
a. Record the final population numbers in the table above.
b. Using two colors, create a key, show the scales on the y-axis, and draw the graphs for the two populations.

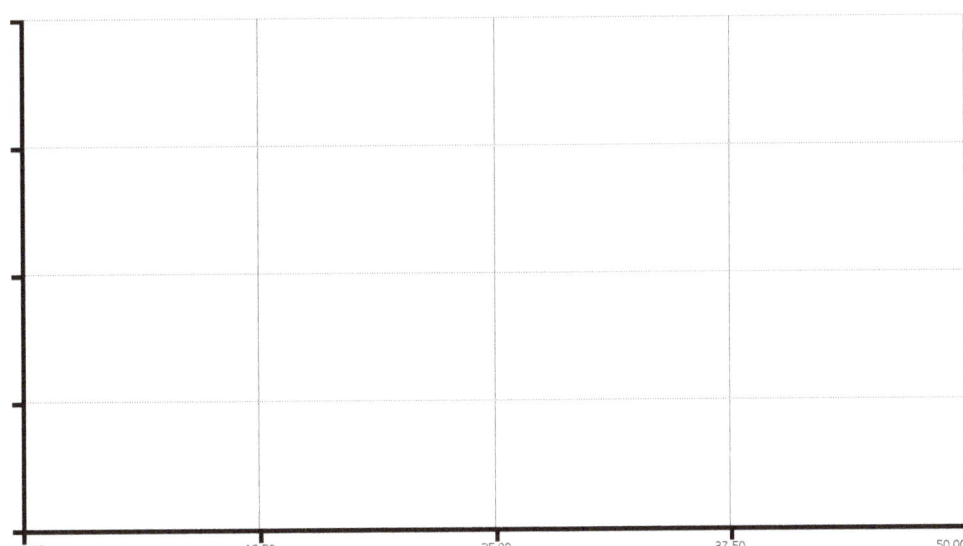

c. Why did the settings you selected create more stable populations over time?

d. Imagine that you are a wildlife manager, working to maintain a healthy ecosystem. Based on your conclusion above, what policies do you recommend be implemented to keep the populations healthy and stable? Make sure to include detail and rationale for each of your policies.

LESSON 4, LEVEL C, HANDOUT 5 – P.1

Predator and Prey Dynamics – Assessment 1

Moose are dependent on the Balsam Fir population for 60% of their diet and any change in Fir density affects Moose density. Add this stock (Fir Trees) and the necessary elements to show this additional part of the Ecosystem on the Island.

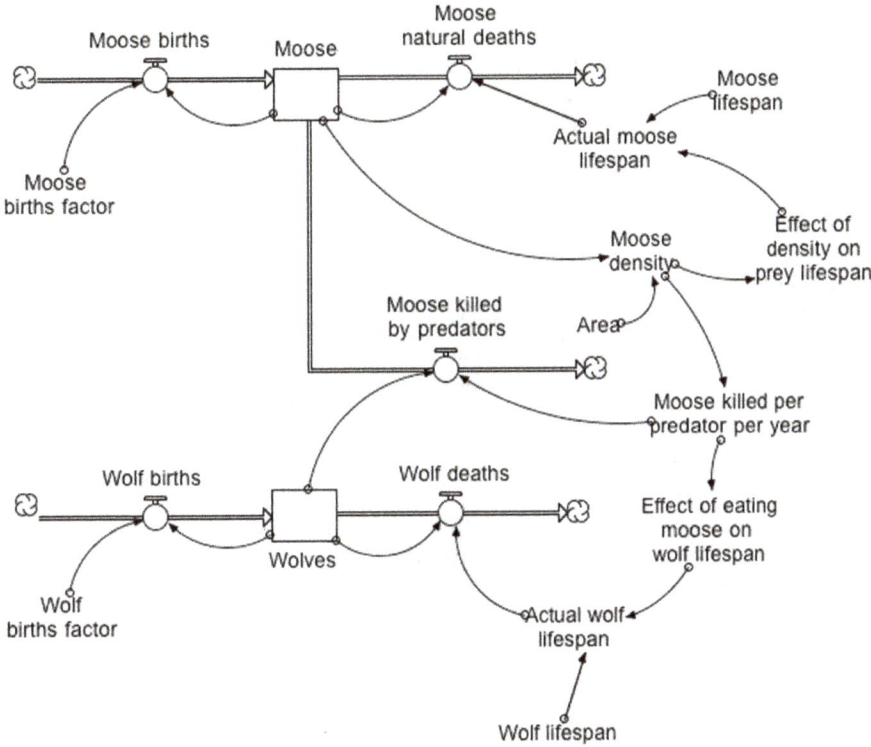

In summary, what story does the map tell about predator, prey, and food relationships?

LESSON 4, LEVEL C, HANDOUT 6 – P.1

Predator and Prey Dynamics – Assessment 2

Moose are dependent on the Balsam Fir population for 60% of their diet and any change in Fir density affects Moose density. Add this stock (Fir Trees) as a box and the necessary elements to show this additional part of the Ecosystem on the Island.

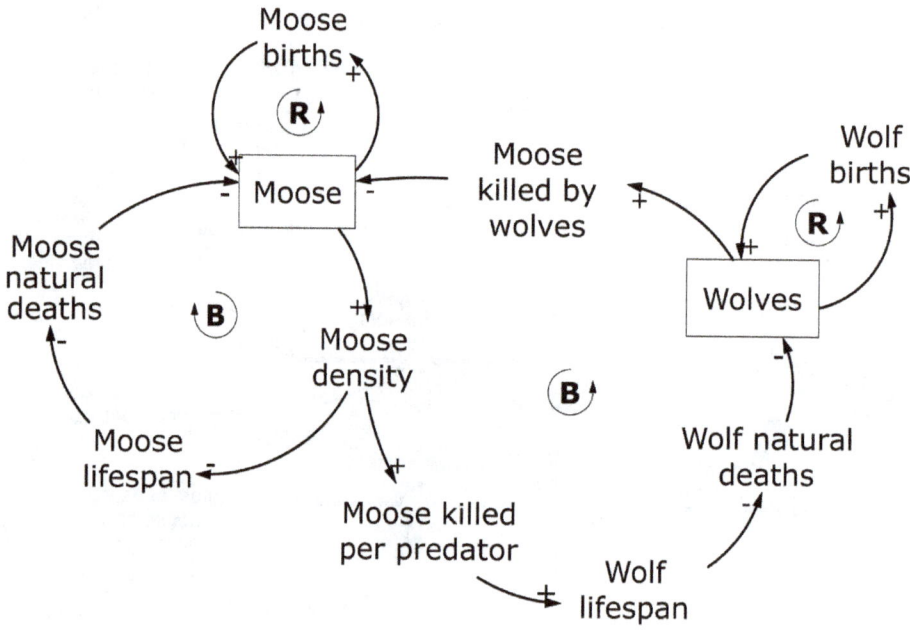

In summary, what story do the loops tell about predator, prey, and food relationships?

Lesson 5 – Level C

Eat and Be Eaten: Prey as Predator, Predator as Prey

Overview

This model explores a moose and wolf population. A predator/prey relationship is present, as with Lesson 4, but now the moose have a food source, creating a more realistic representation of the ecosystem. Students take on the role of wildlife manager and control hunting policies for both predator and prey populations. The default simulation behavior for prey, predators, and biomass is oscillation. Depending on policy decisions, a variety of results occur.

Learning Goals

- Represent and interpret data on a line graph.
- Compare results for simulation runs.
- Manage a simulated ecosystem, keeping it healthy.
- Identify and explain challenges of being a wildlife manager and meeting specific goals.

LESSON 5 – LEVEL C – AGES 13+

Time
Three to four 45-minute sessions

Materials
- One computer for every 2–3 students
- Handouts (See pages 80–94)

Curricular Connections
- Science: Populations, ecosystems, scientific method
- Math: Vary assumptions, explore consequences, and compare predictions with data.*
- Reading: Analyze a complex set of ideas or sequence of events and explain how specific individuals, ideas, or events interact and develop over the course of the text.*

Common Core State Standards

Key system dynamics concepts and insights
- Expanding boundaries can provide a bigger picture of how a system works. (Note: this model adds a food supply for the prey.)
- Systems can have conflicting goals, thus making it difficult to manage system results.
- Balancing feedback loops (predator/prey and prey/biomass) keep the system "in check."

Additional information

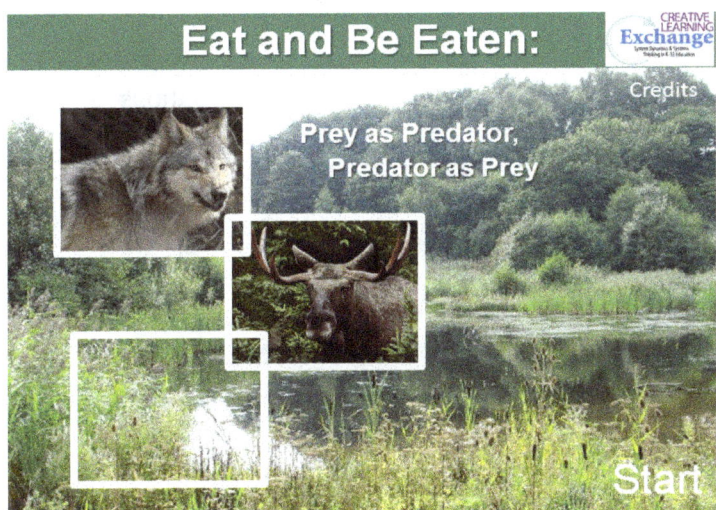

FIGURE 1: Title Screen

Student Challenge

Keep the ecosystem healthy while managing related human interests, even in the face of unexpected events such as a drought.

Lesson Details

Preparation

1. Create groups of 2–3 students each.
2. Check computers to make sure you can access the online simulation.
3. Copy each handout double-sided for each student. See the chart below to determine how many copies of each handout you'll need.

#	Page	Handout	Description
1	80–82	Introduction	This section includes instructions for assembling a learning portfolio and an assessment rubric. Students then get started on the simulation using step-by-step directions.
2	83–84	Baseline Run with experimental exploration	Students set up and record the data for a baseline run. They then explore "What if?" questions, recording their data for the best run.
3	85–89	Challenge Runs	Students work to complete two specific ecosystem challenges.
4	90–91	Debrief	Students step through the debrief and write their reflections.
5	92–94	Recommendation (Official Memo)	Students create a final analysis of the data, make recommendations, and write a summary for the forest director.

4. *Optional:* You may want to read the background information about the underlying structure of the model. This can be useful as you guide students to understanding the model behavior as it relates to real-world behaviors and the limitations of the model. (Eat and Be Eaten Model Background Info available as a separate file http://www.clexchange.org/ftp/documents/x-curricular/CC2012_Oscillations5BackgroundInformation.pdf)

Lesson Sequence

1. Introduce students to any specific content knowledge related to ecosystems, animal populations, etc., that you'd like students to have prior to running the simulation. This may include definitions of terms such as: ecosystem, lifespan, area, population density, predator, prey, nutritional needs, and biomass.

2. Have students open the simulation and work through the simulation introduction, runs, and debrief using the guided handouts. Note that the handouts guide students through the simulation in a step-by-step manner. If you'd like to leave the exploration more open, then you may eliminate some of the handouts. Figure 2 shows the control panel screen.

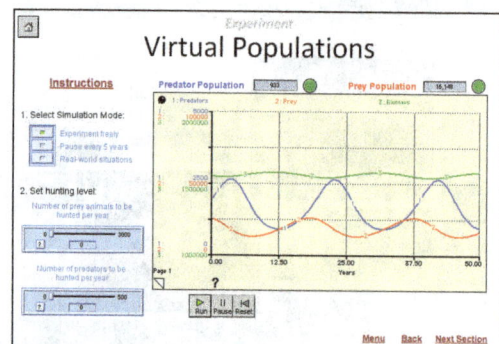

FIGURE 2: Control Panel

Debrief and Assessment

1. Using the instructions and rubric, have students assemble their portfolios and write up their recommendations and summary.

2. One option is to ask students to orally present their recommendations within small groups or in front of the class. Peers could ask questions and give feedback to one another using aspects of the same rubric.
3. Debrief the simulation experience as a class, using ideas for bringing the lesson home.

Assessment Ideas

Using a rubric, students assemble a portfolio of their learning. The portfolio includes a recommendation to the park director (the boss) explaining a plan of action and the rationale for choosing it.

Bringing the Lesson Home

Discuss these and any other questions that have surfaced about model behaviors.
- How does the addition of a food source for the prey impact the dynamics of the ecosystem?
- Why do the prey start dying from starvation before the biomass is completely gone?
- To what degree should human interests impact ecosystem policy decisions?
- How might differing needs from various parts of the system (animals, plants, hunters, farmers, and residents) make it difficult to manage a system over time?

ACKNOWLEDGEMENTS

Lesson 5 – Level C • Eat and Be Eaten: Prey as Predator, Predator as Prey
©2014 Creative Learning Exchange
www.clexchange.org

This model with accompanying lesson is one in a series that explores the characteristics of complex systems.

Model created with contributions from Jen Andersen, Anne LaVigne, Michael Radzicki, George Richardson, Lees Stuntz, and with support from Jay Forrester and the Creative Learning Exchange.

Image Sources and Credits
The following images are in the public domain:
Wolf - Source: http://earthjustice.org/features/campaigns/wolf-recovery-under-attack-in-the-northern-rockies; author Gary Kramer, US Fish and Wildlife Service
Moose - Source: http://www.northshorenature.org/exhibits/mammals.php?pageNum_recordsCritters=2&totalRows_recordsCritters=5; US Fish and Wildlife Service
Poison Ivy - Source: http://commons.wikimedia.org/wiki/File:Toxicodendron_radicans.jpg; author Esculapio
Creative Commons Attribution-ShareAlike 3.0 Unported license (http://creativecommons.org/licenses/by-sa/3.0/deed.en) on either Wikipedia.org or Wikimedia Commons:

Trophic pyramid - Source: http://commons.wikimedia.org/wiki/File: TrophicWeb.jpg; author Thompsma
Creative Commons Attribution-Share Alike 2.5 Generic license (http://creativecommons.org/licenses/by-sa/2.5/deed.en) on Wikimedia Commons:
Caterpillar - Source: http://commons.wikimedia.org/wiki/File:Plain_tiger_moat.JPG; author Viren Vaz
Creative Commons Attribution-Share Alike 2.0 Generic license (http://creativecommons.org/licenses/by-sa/2.0/deed.en) on Wikimedia Commons:
Plant with Insect - Source: http://commons.wikimedia.org/wiki/File:Drosera_capensis_bend.JPG; author Noah Elhardt
Balsam Fir, USDA, Public Domain

Eat and Be Eaten – Introduction

You are a new employee of a major national park and will be in charge of issuing hunting licenses and deciding whether or not to allow predators to be killed if humans or their animals are at risk. In preparation for taking on this role, you will run a simulation to determine how different policies play out over time. You'll explore the sections (in **bold**) as indicated. Remember, you can always revisit a section anytime you like.

After running this "Training Simulator," you will write up a recommendation to your boss (the park director) explaining your plan and your rationale for choosing it. The park director will score your recommendation and portfolio with a rubric (see next page).

At the conclusion of this project, you will need the following items organized into a portfolio.

1. Title page that incorporates the following:
   - Title: Wildlife Management Project Analysis
   - Your name
   - One or more drawings, illustrations, and/or diagrams that illustrate what you learned

2. Your "Official Memo" (Handout 5) to the forest director, Rutheforest T. Grove

3. Handouts 1–4, complete and organized neatly in order:
   - Handout 1 – Instructions, Rubric, and Introduction
   - Handout 2 – Baseline Run
   - Handout 3 – Challenge Runs
   - Handout 4 – Debrief
   - Handout 5 – Official Memo

Project Assessment Rubric

	Novice	Basic	Proficient	Advanced
Title	Little to no visuals are included.	Visuals are included, but they are not clearly linked to learning.	Visual representations clearly show key learning.	In addition, a diagram clearly shows cause and effect relationships.
Ecosystem Health	The ecosystem is completely out of balance (e.g., all of the predators are gone).	The ecosystem is somewhat out of balance (e.g., populations have big ups and downs over time).	The ecosystem is stable and healthy.	In addition to having a healthy ecosystem, the hunters, residents, and farmers are satisfied with your job performance.
Data (within the simulation handouts and in the recommendation)	Little to no data is included.	Some data is included, but it is not clear or accurately recorded.	The recorded data is relevant, accurate and clearly represented.	In addition to the data, the analysis shows logical connections to the hunter and farmer/resident satisfaction over time.
Explanations (within the simulation handouts and in the recommendation)	Little to no explanation of the data is included.	Some explanation of the data is included, but it includes little detail and has some inaccuracies.	Explanations are clear and link directly to the data on the graphs.	In addition, explanations describe trends and inter-connections.
Recommendations (RECs) and Rationale	RECs are missing or unclear.	RECs are present but not clearly linked to the data analysis.	RECs are clearly linked to the data analysis.	In addition, RECs include subtleties that are not explicitly shown in the data but are inferred from the data.

	Novice	**Basic**	**Proficient**	**Advanced**
Summary and Conclusions	Summary and/or conclusion is missing.	Summary and policy statement are included but are unclear or inaccurate.	Brings together the data and recommendations into a concise summary and a general policy statement.	In addition, includes a rationale for why you will be best able to manage the forest as a new employee.

Introduction
Open web address: http://www.clexchange.org/curriculum/complexsystems/oscillation/
Select the **Waves of Change: Predator and Prey Dynamics-Level C** simulation and **click "Start."**

1. Click <u>Introduction – Wildlife Manager.</u>

a. What is an ecosystem?

b. What do you think it means to be a wildlife manager?

Click <u>Read more about your area</u>

c. Why might an ecosystem be referred to as an island if it isn't surrounded by water?

d. What are some current concerns relating to the wolf population?

e. What are some current concerns relating to the moose population?

f. Define the term "biomass" and explain why it is important within this ecosystem.

g. What is a "boom and bust" cycle?

Click <u>Menu.</u>
2. Click <u>Experiment with the Model.</u>
You will use the following worksheets to predict and record your virtual experiments.

LESSON 5, LEVEL C, HANDOUT 2 – P.1

Eat and Be Eaten – Run #1: Baseline Run

Click on the **?** button for each of the sliders to see what each one does. Input the values shown below onto the simulation screen, but don't run it just yet.

Simulation Mode	Experiment freely
Prey hunting	0
Predator hunting	0

Predict: What do you think will happen to the two populations and the biomass?

Draw your general prediction as lines on the graph, showing the predators, the prey, and the biomass in three different colors. Now **click** "Run."

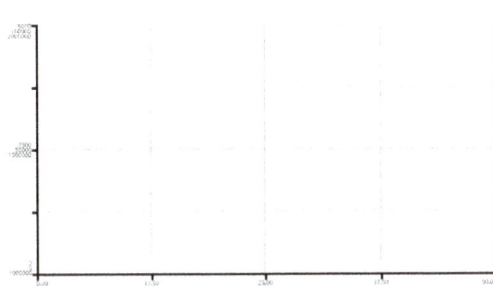

Analysis:
a. Using the same three colors, create a key, label the appropriate scales on the y-axis with the respective colors, and draw the three lines on the graph below.

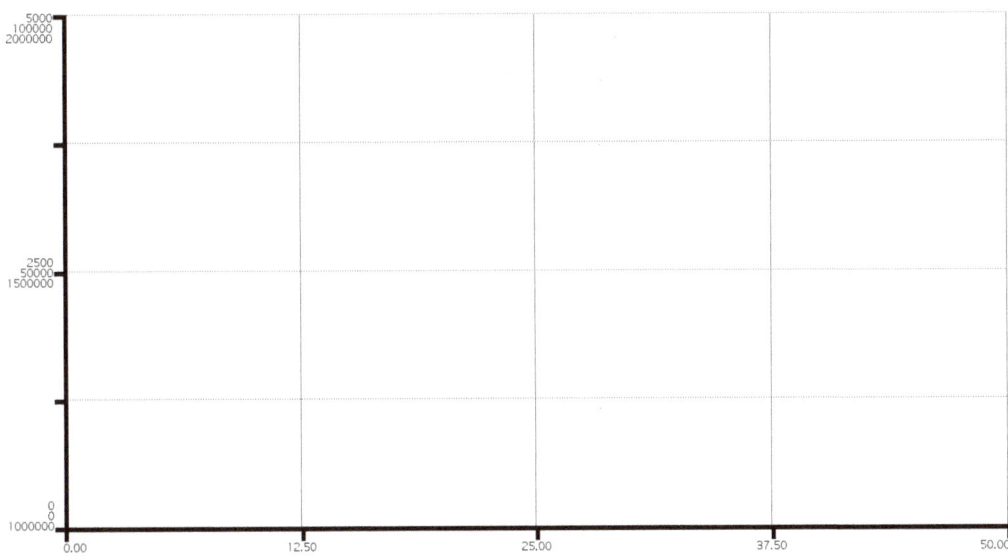

©2014 Creative Learning Exchange

b. Explain why you think the populations and biomass changed as they did. Make sure to discuss how and why the populations and biomass impacted one another.
Optional: Include a visual representation of the relationships between the predator, prey, and biomass.

c. Continue your exploration, asking "What if" questions, keeping the model in the "experiment freely" mode. Ask one question at a time, running the simulator until you have a feel for the behavior that is being produced.

Example questions:
Question 1: What might happen if I allow some hunting of prey?
Question 2: What might happen if I allow some predators to be killed?
Question 3: What might happen if I allow both prey hunting and predator kills?
Question 4: What might happen if I allow a very high level of hunting either predators or prey or both?

d. Write a brief summary of what you've learned so far.

LESSON 5, LEVEL C, HANDOUT 3 – P.1

Eat and Be Eaten – Challenge Runs
Challenge Run #1: Can you keep the ecosystem in balance?

Set the simulation mode to "Pause every 5 years."
Set up your initial hunting for year 0, click "Run," and then make changes as needed every time the simulation pauses. Record your settings as you go in the table.

Year	Prey Hunting	Predator Hunting
0		
5		
10		
15		
20		
25		
30		
35		
40		

Analysis:
a. Using the same three colors, create a key, label the appropriate scales on the y-axis with the respective colors, and draw the three lines on the graph below.

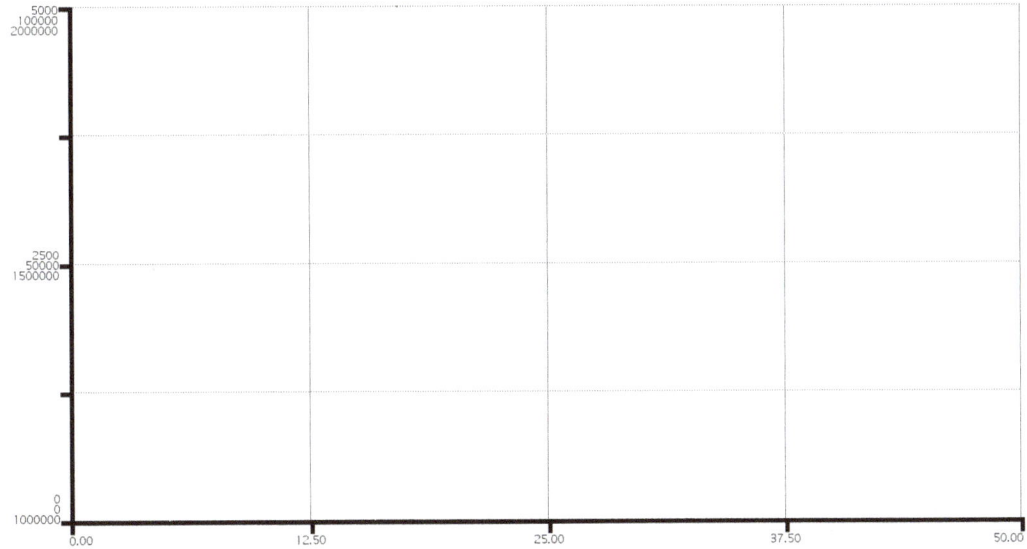

©2014 Creative Learning Exchange

b. What was your general strategy, and how successful were you in achieving stable (flat-line) population levels over time?

c. What changes would you make to improve your results?

Continue running the simulation in pause mode, trying different hunting strategies. Record your best run and explain what you did to achieve those results.

Year	Prey Hunting	Predator Hunting
0		
5		
10		
15		
20		
25		
30		
35		
40		

Analysis:
Using the same three colors, create a key, label the appropriate scales on the y-axis with the respective colors, and draw the three lines on the graph below.

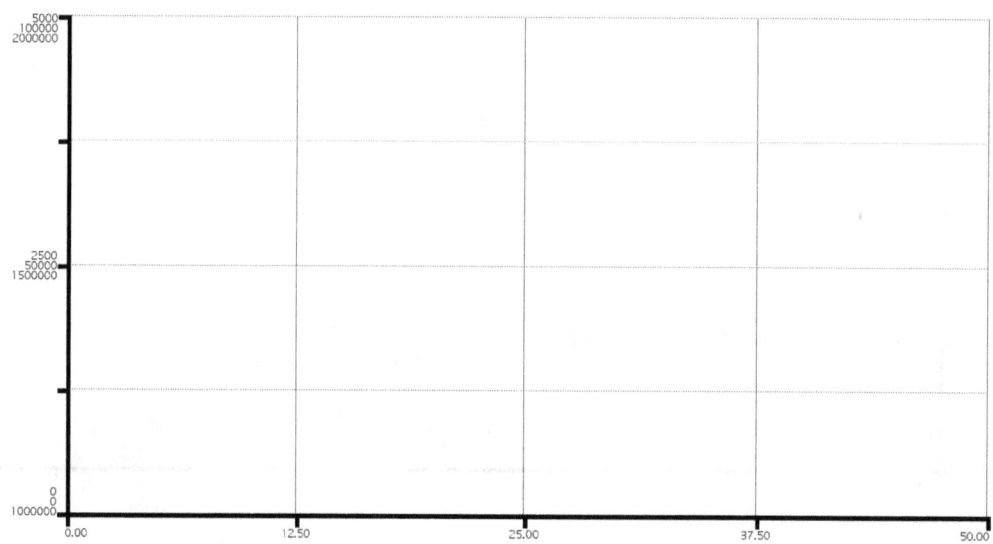

Challenge Run #2: Can you keep the ecosystem in balance while meeting the needs of the hunters, residents, and farmers?

Set the simulation mode to "Real-world situations." Set up your initial hunting for year 0, click "Run," and then make changes as needed. You can pause whenever you like to make changes. Record the year, messages, and your settings in the table. You can see the year (time) by pointing and clicking on the end of the graph line.

Year	Message Issue	Prey Hunting	Predator Hunting
0	None		

Analysis:

a. Using the same three colors, create a key, label the appropriate scales on the y-axis with the respective colors, and draw the three lines on the graph below.

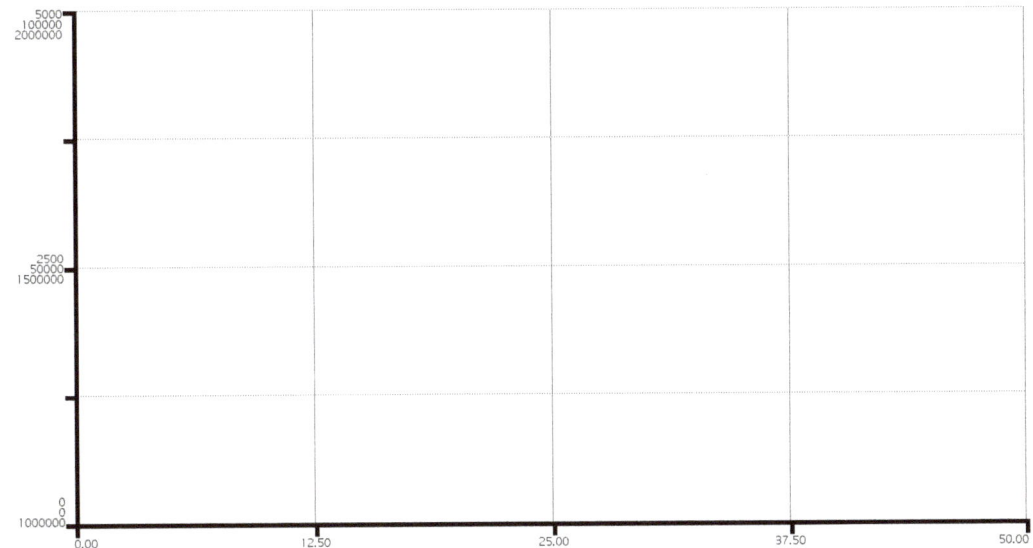

b. What was your general strategy and how successful were you in achieving stable (flat-line) population levels over time?

c. **Click** the triangle (bottom left on graph pad) to flip to "Page 5." Looking at this graph that shows the number of prey killed by hunters and the number of prey hunters wanted to kill, how satisfied do you think the hunters are? Draw the graph lines and your perception of the hunters' satisfaction level (using three new colors).

Prey Killed vs. Desired Prey Killed   Hunter Satisfaction

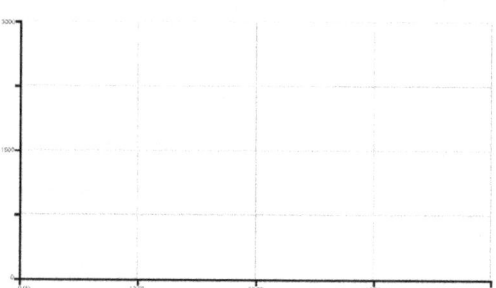   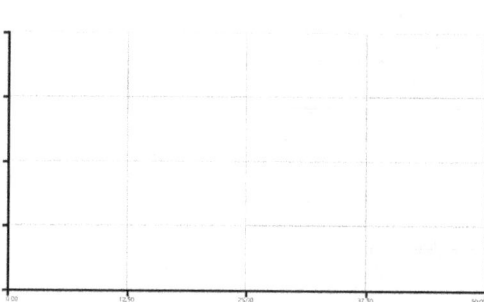

d. Based on all three graph lines above, why do you think that the hunters might feel this way?

e. Based on the graph of predators and any messages you received, how do you think the farmers and residents were feeling over time?

f. What changes would you make to improve your results?

Continue running the simulation in "Real-world situations" mode, trying different hunting strategies. Record your best run and explain what you did to achieve those results on a blank sheet of paper.

Year	Message Issue	Prey Hunting	Predator Hunting
0	None		

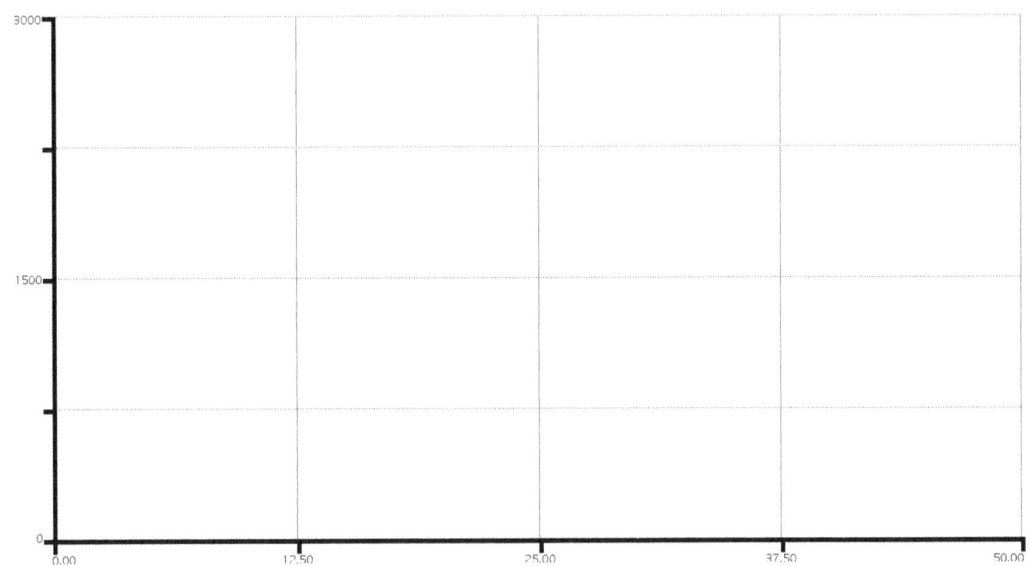

Predators, Prey, and Biomass Graph

Prey Killed vs. Desired Prey Killed

Hunter Satisfaction

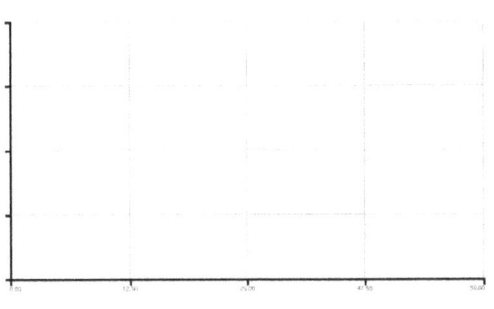

LESSON 5, LEVEL C, HANDOUT 4 – P.1

Eat and Be Eaten – Debrief

Click Menu and then **Debrief Central.** You'll go through each of these sections of the debrief to process what you experienced in the simulation.

Click A. Behavior Patterns.
Read and click on What's really happening.
a. Why is the situation reflected in this graph not an ideal situation for the health of the ecosystem? Make sure to include thoughts about all parts of the ecosystem in your explanation.

Click Continue. Read and click on What's really happening.
b. Why do you, or don't you, think this result is successful management?

c. How would the hunters feel over time? Why?

Click Menu and **B. Explore the Model.**
Read "Model as Hypothesis" and answer the following:

a. How do the three main parts of the ecosystem (predators, prey, and biomass) affect one another?

LESSON 5, LEVEL C, HANDOUT 4 – P.2

Click Tour the Model Structure. Use the space bar to see one piece added at a time.
b. Looking at the map of the system, fill in the following table.

Stock	What increases the stock?	What decreases the stock?	How does this stock affect another stock(s)?
Predator Population			
Prey Population			
Biomass			

Click Tour the Loops. **Click** on the B (Balancing) and R (Reinforcing) symbols for the explanations. **Click** "More Loops" and read through these as well.

c. Choose one of the loops, draw it here, and "tell the story" of that loop in your own words.

d. How does that loop relate to the behaviors you saw in the simulation?

Click Menu and then **C. Connections.**
Click on each of the models and read about the purpose of using a model to better understand predator, prey, and biomass interactions.
List and describe one or more situations that might be better understood with a model.

Situation	How a model could increase understanding

©2014 Creative Learning Exchange

LESSON 5, LEVEL C, HANDOUT 5 – P.1

Eat and Be Eaten – Official Memo

DATE:

TO: Rutheforest T. Grove, Park Director

FROM:

REGARDING: Official Management Recommendation

Data and Analysis:

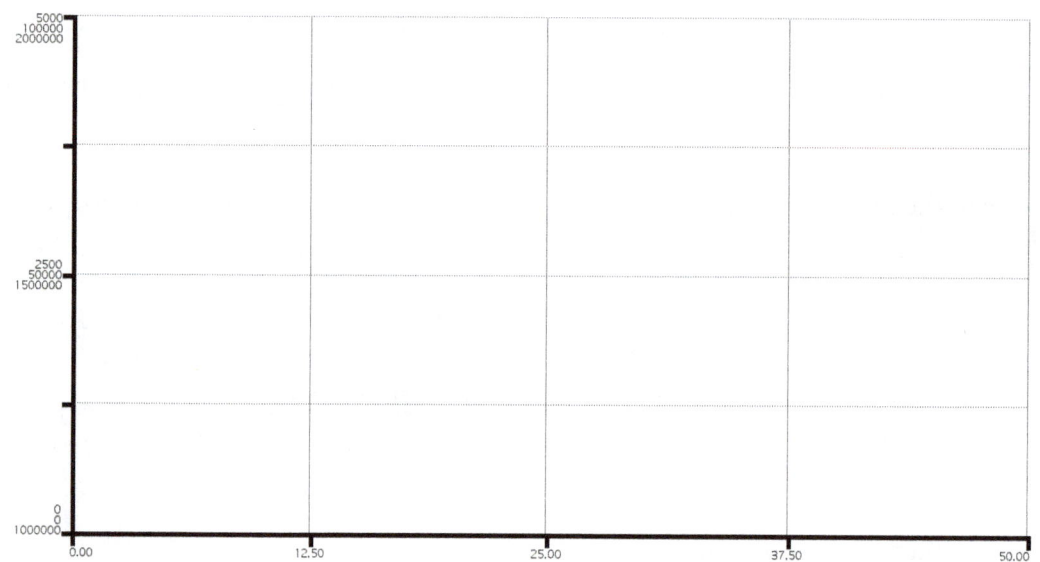

FIGURE 1: Graph of stable simulated ecosystem (predators, prey, biomass)

Actions that led to this result:

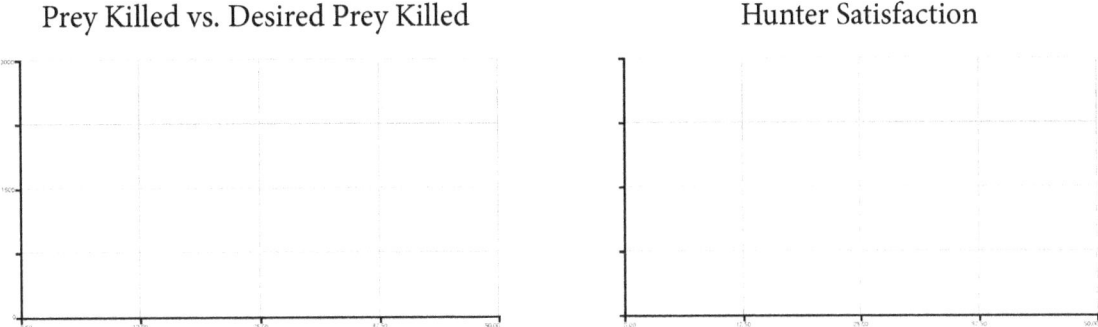

FIGURE 2: Graphs of acceptable hunting levels for predators and prey

Year	Complaint and Issues	Action Taken

FIGURE 3: Complaints from hunters and farmers/residents

Actions that best led to keeping the surrounding community members satisfied, while at the same time keeping the ecosystem healthy:

FIGURE 4: Recommendations

Policy Areas	Recommendations	Rationale (Why this policy is good for the ecosystem and the surrounding community)
#1 – Hunting Prey		
#2 – Hunting Predators		
#3 – Responding to Complaints from Hunters		
#4 – Responding to Complaints from Farmers/ Residents		

Summary and General Conclusions: (Attach additional supporting documents)

Lesson 6 – Level C

The Big Squeeze: Pressure, Achievement and Burnout

Overview

This model illustrates a workaholic situation where pressure is entirely internally generated through increasing one's own expectations for oneself. Overachievers can understand how setting the bar ever higher can be unhealthy behavior over the long-term even though they have been successful with this strategy so far in life.

Learning Goals

- Represent and interpret data on a line graph.
- Explore possible causes of burnout and identify potential leverage for prevention.
- Give advice to peers, based on an understanding of causes of burnout and leverage points.
- Self-assess, reflect, and make a personal plan.

FIGURE 1: Title Screen

Student Challenge

While working as a volunteer peer advisor at school, give advice to peers who are experiencing burnout cycles, based on evidence from the simulation.

LESSON 6 – LEVEL C – AGES 13+

Time
Three to four 45-minute sessions

Materials
- One computer for every 2–3 students
- Handouts (See pages 98–116)

Curricular Connections
- Math: Vary assumptions, explore consequences, and compare predictions with data.*
- Science: Feedback mechanisms, motivation of organisms
- Social Studies: Individual development and identity

Common Core State Standards

Key system dynamics concepts and insights
- Being overly driven by accomplishments can set the stage for burnout.
- Inadequate achievement (real or perceived) creates pressure on individuals.
- The body system can break down; prolonged exposure to stress can hinder achievement of goals, adding to even more stress.
- A person can accomplish more in the long-term by limiting what he does in the short-term.

Additional information

Lesson Details

Preparation

1. Create groups of 2–3 students each.
2. Check computers to make sure you can access the online simulation.
3. Copy each handout double-sided for each student. See the chart below to determine how many copies of each handout you'll need.

#	Page	Handout	Description
1	98–100	Introduction	This section includes instructions for assembling a learning portfolio and an assessment rubric. Students then get started on the simulation using step-by-step directions.
2	101–111	Exploration, Peers, and Self	Students explore the settings and results of the simulation. They then start "coaching" students in various situations.
3	112–114	Debrief	Students step through the debrief and write their reflections.
4	115–116	Recommendation	Students create a final analysis of the data, make recommendations, and write a summary for the head advisor.

4. *Optional*: You may want to read the background information about the underlying structure of the model. This can be useful as you guide students to understanding the model behavior as it relates to real-world behaviors and the limitations of the model. (The Big Squeeze Model Background Info available as a separate file http://www.clexchange.org/ftp/documents/x-curricular/CC2012_Oscillations6BackgroundInformation.pdf)

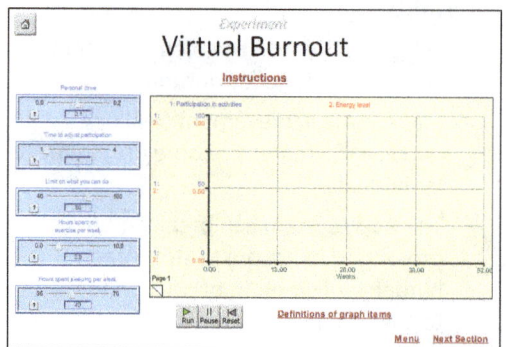

FIGURE 2: Control Panel

Lesson Sequence

1. Introduce students to any specific content knowledge related to burnout that you'd like students to have prior to running the simulation. This may include definitions of terms such as burnout, gaps (between desired accomplishments, perceived accomplishments, and actual accomplishments), internal and external pressures, tradeoffs, and workaholism.

2. Have students open the simulation and work through the simulation introduction, runs, and debrief using the guided handouts. Note that the handouts guide students through the simulation in a step-by-step manner. If you'd like to leave the exploration more open, then you may eliminate some of the handouts. Figure 2 shows the control panel screen.

Debrief and Assessment

1. Using the instructions and rubric, have students assemble their portfolios and write up their recommendations and summary.

2. One option is to ask students to present their recommendations orally within small groups or in front of the class. Peers could ask questions and give feedback to one another using aspects of the same rubric.

3. Debrief the simulation experience as a class, using ideas for bringing the lesson home.

Bringing the Lesson Home

Discuss these and any other questions/topics that surface about model behaviors.

Assessment Ideas
Using a rubric, students assemble a portfolio of their learning. The portfolio includes a report to the head advisor.

- Discuss the three categories of typical causes presented in the simulation – work-related causes, lifestyle causes and personality traits.
- What is a situation in which you've felt "burned out?" What happened and why as a result? What, if anything, in this simulation could relate to your example?
- What would you consider to be more important to preventing burnout – making changes to one's schedule (doing less) or trying to control one's expectations of what can be accomplished (expecting less)? Why?
- Do you think people in different countries experience burnout at different rates and/or for different reasons? Why or why not?
- What other factors not included in the model could be at work in creating burnout?

ACKNOWLEDGEMENTS

Lesson 6 – Level C • The Big Squeeze: Pressure, Achievement and Burnout
©2014 Creative Learning Exchange
www.clexchange.org

This model with accompanying lesson is one in a series that explores the characteristics of complex systems. Model created with contributions from Jen Andersen, Anne LaVigne, Michael Radzicki, George Richardson, Lees Stuntz, and with support from Jay Forrester and the Creative Learning Exchange.

Image Sources and Credits
The following images are in the public domain:
The Scream - Source: http://en.wikipedia.org/wiki/File:The_Scream.jpg; image of painting by Edvard Munch
Mensa connections - Source: http://commons.wikimedia.org/wiki/File:Mensa_Connections.JPG; author Fitzftz

Balance rocks - Source: http://commons.wikimedia.org/wiki/File:Balance_rocks.jpg; author Seventhrunner
Green office space - Source: http://commons.wikimedia.org/wiki/File:Green-office-space.jpg; author Frits Ahlefeldt

The following images are used under the Creative Commons Attribution-ShareAlike 3.0 Unported license (http://creativecommons.org/licenses/by-sa/3.0/deed.en) on either Wikipedia.org or Wikimedia Commons
Earth - Source: http://commons.wikimedia.org/wiki/File:Earths.jpg; author Stephen Slade Tien
Rock climbers - Source: http://commons.wikimedia.org/wiki/File:Uphill_quarry_climbers.jpg; author Geof Sheppard

The following image is used under the Creative Commons Attribution-Share Alike 2.5 Generic license (http://creativecommons.org/licenses/by-sa/2.5/deed.en) on Wikimedia Commons:
Match - Source: http://commons.wikimedia.org/wiki/File:Streichholz.jpg; author Sebastian Ritter

The following images are used under the Creative Commons Attribution 2.0 Generic license (http://creativecommons.org/licenses/by/2.0/deed.en) on Wikimedia Commons:
Internet sign - Source: http://commons.wikimedia.org/wiki/File:Internet-Sign.jpg; author cawi2001
Thailand beach - Source: http://commons.wikimedia.org/wiki/File:Sunset_at_Patong_beach_Phuket_Thailand.jpg; author Rene Ehrhardt

The Big Squeeze – Introduction

You are volunteering as a peer coach in your school. Part of your new role is to listen to students who are having trouble keeping their lives in balance because they are either taking on too much work or not enough work. In preparation for taking on this role, you will run a simulation to determine how different policies play out over time. You'll explore the sections (in bold) as indicated. Remember, you can always revisit a section anytime you like.

After finishing your first day on the job, you will write up a recommendation to the head advisor, Mrs. Darcy, explaining your plan and your rationale for choosing it. The advisor will score your recommendation and portfolio with a rubric (see next page).

At the conclusion of this project, you will need the following elements organized into a portfolio.

1. Title page that incorporates the following:
   - Title: The Big Squeeze: Pressure, Achievement and Burnout
   - Your name
   - One or more drawings, illustrations, and/or diagrams that illustrate life choices related to school, work, and play. You can create a collage, drawing, or other representation to show the parts of the system and how they are connected.

2. Your report to Mrs. Darcy (Handout 4), documenting the following:
   - Students you met with and advice you gave
   - Summary page with key learnings and general conclusions (with evidence)

3. Handouts 1–3, complete and organized neatly in order
   - Handout 1 – Instructions, Rubric, and Introduction
   - Handout 2 – Exploration, Peer Runs, and My Pattern
   - Handout 3 – Debrief

Project Assessment Rubric

	Novice	Basic	Proficient	Advanced
Title	Little to no visuals are included.	Visuals are included, but they are not clearly linked to the system.	Visual representations clearly show key aspects of the system.	In addition, a diagram clearly shows cause-and-effect relationships.
Data (within the simulation handouts and in the recommendation)	Little to no data is included.	Some data is included, but it is not clear or accurately recorded.	The recorded data is relevant, accurate and clearly represented.	In addition to the data, the report describes logical connections between the data and conclusions.
Explanations (within the simulation handouts and in the recommendation)	Little to no explanation of the data is included.	Some explanation of the data is included, but it includes little detail and has some inaccuracies.	Explanations are clear and directly linked to the data on the graphs.	In addition, explanations describe trends and interconnections.
Recommendations (RECs) and Rationale	RECs are missing or unclear.	RECs are present but not clearly linked to the data analysis.	RECs are clearly linked to the data analysis.	In addition, RECs include subtleties that are not explicitly shown in the data, but are inferred from the data.

LESSON 6, LEVEL C, HANDOUT 1 – P.3

	Novice	Basic	Proficient	Advanced
Summary and Conclusions	Summary and/or conclusions are missing.	Summary is included but is unclear or inaccurate.	Data and recommendations are brought together into a concise summary.	In addition, the summary includes a rationale for why certain choices best prevent burnout cycles.

Introduction

Open web address: http://www.clexchange.org/curriculum/complexsystems/oscillation/
Select **The Big Squeeze: Pressure, Achievement and Burnout-Level C** simulation and **click**, "Start."

Click 1. Introduction – Burnout Dynamics.

Read the introduction and **click** on the pictures.

a. In your own words, what is burnout? _____
_____

b. What causes burnout? _____
_____

c. What does it mean to be a peer coach in the simulation? _____
_____

d. Give one example of "activity" as defined in the simulation. _____
_____

e. What is an activity that is not included in the definition? _____
_____

Click Menu.
Click 2. Experiment with the Model.

Click the question marks (**?**) on the slidebars and write definitions in your own words.
Personal drive: _____
_____

Time to adjust participation: _____

Limit on what you can do: _____
_____

Hours spent on exercise per week: _____

Hours spent on sleeping per week: _____

100 • LESSON 6 – Level C • The Big Squeeze ©2014 Creative Learning Exchange

The Big Squeeze:
Pressure, Achievement and Burnout – Exploration

Do several runs with different settings. Just experiment and see what you can discover about what happens with different settings. When you feel that you know enough to give your peers some advice, write a summary of your learning below and proceed to your first peer coaching meeting. Make sure to include what causes the ups and downs of burnout in the simulation.

What I've learned so far:
_____
_____
_____
_____
_____
_____
_____
_____
_____
_____
_____
_____
_____
_____
_____
_____
_____
_____
_____
_____
_____
_____
_____
_____

Peer Coaching Schedule:
Peer #1 – Raven
Peer #2 – Sammy
Peer #3 – Evelyn
Peer #4 – Oxford
Reflection: My Pattern

Peer #1 – Raven

Raven is an extremely ambitious student. She will be the first person in her family to attend college, and both she and everyone around her have very high expectations. Because of her drive to do more and more no matter what, she has been having some problems keeping promises over the last year. Her family is very worried because she's always stayed on top of responsibilities in the past.

Set the simulation as shown below and then **Run**.

Slider	Setting
Personal drive	0.2 (very high)
Time to adjust participation	1 week
Limit on what you can do	90 hours/week
Hours spent on exercise per week	2 hours/week
Hours spent sleeping per week	35 hours/week

Record your results on the graphs below. Make sure to create labels and a key for each graph. Note that you'll need to click the bottom-left corner of the graph to see Page 2.

Participation in activities and Energy level

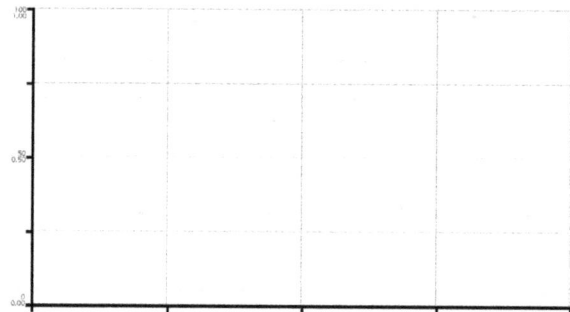

Accomplishments per week, Desired accomplishments per week, and Satisfaction with accomplishments

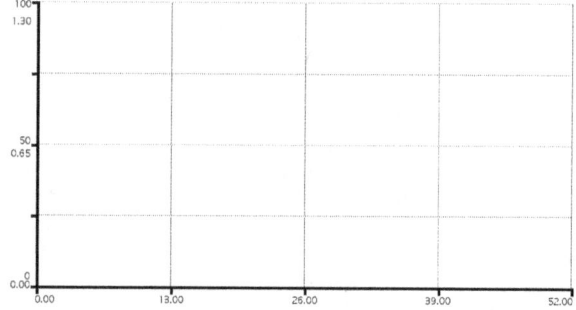

What is happening in the graphs and why?

_____
_____
_____
_____
_____
_____
_____
_____
_____
_____
_____
_____
_____
_____
_____
_____
_____
_____
_____
_____

a. Why do you think Raven is experiencing cycles of burnout?
_____
_____
_____

b. Raven wants to stop the cycles, but she still wants to achieve a lot. What are some ideas that would help her stop the crazy ups and downs, while still keeping accomplishments high?
_____
_____
_____

Continue running the simulation, trying different plans for Raven. Record the graphs for your best run below.

Participation in activities and Energy level

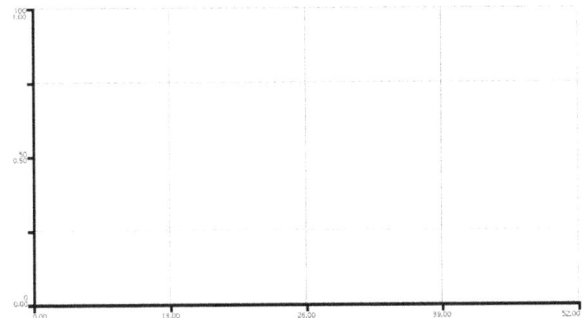

Accomplishments per week, Desired accomplishments per week, and Satisfaction with accomplishments

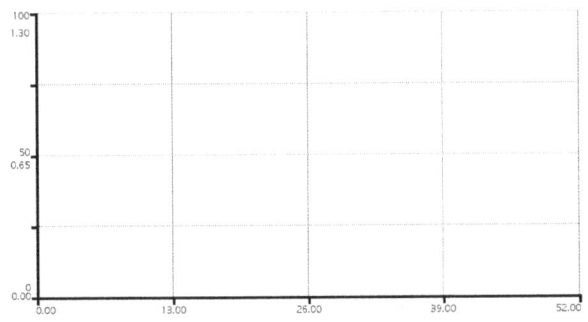

c. What are the new settings?

Slider	Setting
Personal drive	
Time to adjust participation	
Limit on what you can do	
Hours spent on exercise per week	
Hours spent sleeping per week	

d. What changes would Raven really need to make in her life in order to accomplish this?
_____
_____
_____
_____
_____
_____
_____

Peer #2 – Sammy

Sammy has high drive, but he also finds time to exercise, and he gets plenty of sleep. His goal is to make the next Olympics team in gymnastics. Unfortunately, he still has times of exhaustion. This causes him to lose interest in working so hard; he stops showing up for practice and is also having trouble keeping up in school.

Set the simulation as shown below and then **Run**.

Slider	Setting
Personal drive	0.2 (very high)
Time to adjust participation	1 week
Limit on what you can do	100 hours/week
Hours spent on exercise per week	10 hours/week
Hours spent sleeping per week	60 hours/week

Record your results on the graphs below. Make sure to create labels and a key for each graph. Note that you'll need to click the bottom-left corner of the graph to see Page 2.

Participation in activities and Energy level

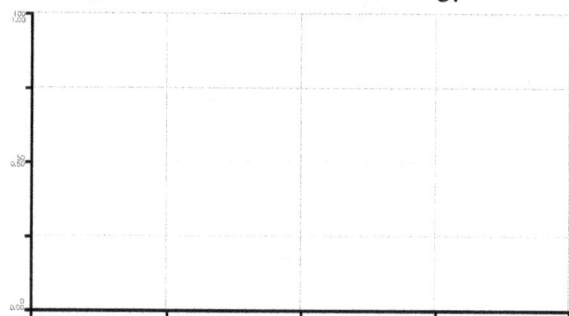

Accomplishments per week, Desired accomplishments per week, and Satisfaction with accomplishments

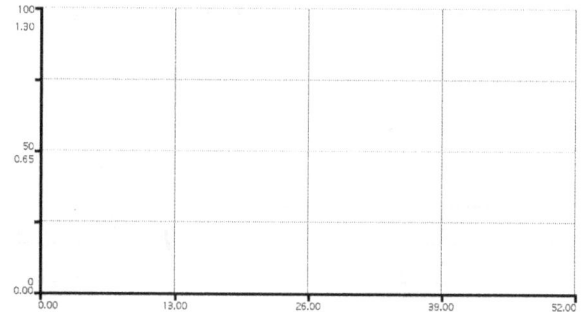

What is happening in the graphs and why?

_____
_____
_____
_____
_____
_____
_____
_____
_____
_____
_____
_____
_____
_____
_____
_____
_____
_____
_____
_____

LESSON 6, LEVEL C, HANDOUT 2 – P.4

a. Why do you think Sammy is experiencing cycles of burnout?
_____
_____
_____

b. Sammy wants to stop the cycles, but he still wants to make the team. What are some ideas that would help him stop the crazy ups and downs, while still keeping his chances high for making the Olympics team?
_____
_____
_____

Continue running the simulation, trying different plans for Sammy. Record the graphs for your best run below.

Participation in activities and Energy level

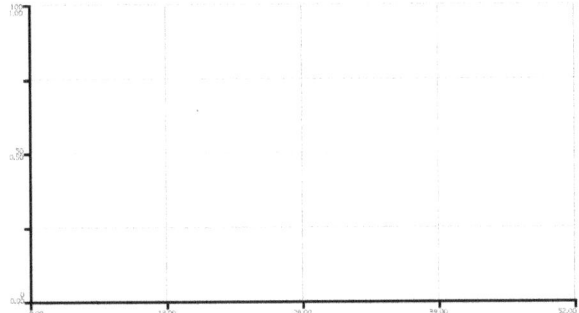

Accomplishments per week, Desired accomplishments per week, and Satisfaction with accomplishments

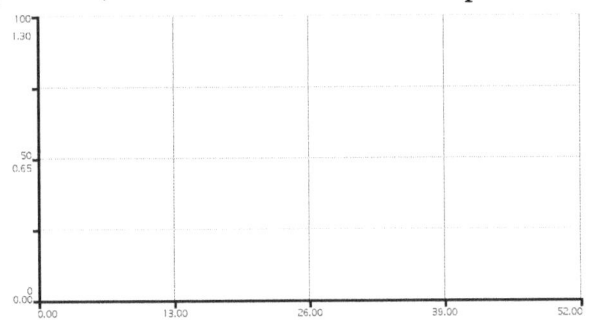

c. What are the new settings?

Slider	Setting
Personal drive	
Time to adjust participation	
Limit on what you can do	
Hours spent on exercise per week	
Hours spent sleeping per week	

d. What changes would Sammy really need to make in his life in order to accomplish this?
_____
_____
_____
_____
_____
_____
_____

©2014 Creative Learning Exchange   LESSON 6 – Level C • The Big Squeeze • 105

LESSON 6, LEVEL C, HANDOUT 2 – P.5

Peer #3 – Evelyn
Evelyn has some drive and she has a hard time saying no to other people's requests. Because of this, her participation limit is high. She doesn't find the time to exercise because she is always doing tasks for other people.

Set the simulation as shown below and then **Run**.

Slider	Setting
Personal drive	0.1 (some)
Time to adjust participation	1 week
Limit on what you can do	80 hours/week
Hours spent on exercise per week	0 hours/week
Hours spent sleeping per week	40 hours/week

Record your results on the graphs below. Make sure to create labels and a key for each graph. Note that you'll need to click the bottom-left corner of the graph to see Page 2.

Participation in activities and Energy level

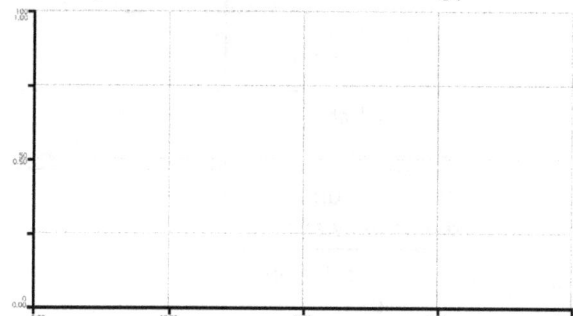

Accomplishments per week, Desired accomplishments per week, and Satisfaction with accomplishments

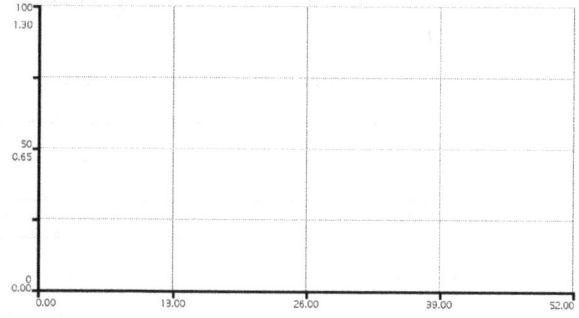

What is happening in the graphs and why?

_____
_____
_____
_____
_____
_____
_____
_____
_____
_____
_____
_____
_____
_____
_____
_____
_____
_____
_____
_____

a. Why do you think Evelyn is experiencing cycles of burnout?
___
___
___

b. Evelyn wants to stop the cycles, but she still wants to achieve a lot. What are some ideas that would help her stop the crazy ups and downs, while still letting her help out others from time to time?
___
___
___

Continue running the simulation, trying different plans for Evelyn. Record the graphs for your best run below.

Participation in activities and Energy level

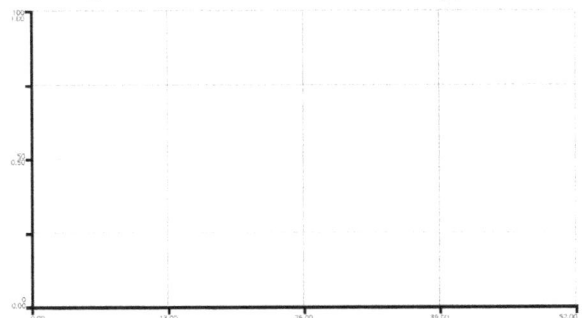

Accomplishments per week, Desired accomplishments per week, and Satisfaction with accomplishments

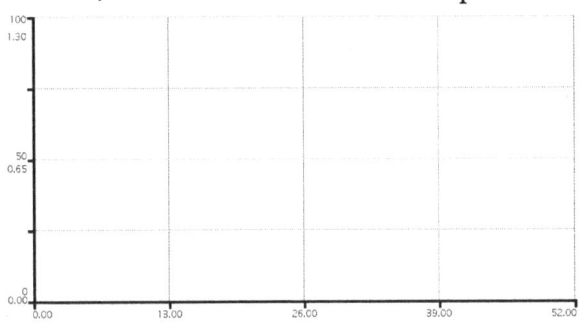

c. What are the new settings?

Slider	Setting
Personal drive	
Time to adjust participation	
Limit on what you can do	
Hours spent on exercise per week	
Hours spent sleeping per week	

d. What changes would Evelyn really need to make in her life in order to accomplish this?
___
___
___
___
___
___
___

Peer #4 – Oxford

Oxford has no drive at the moment. He wants to do more than he's currently doing, but he could use some advice. He does not want to turn his life into "Work, Work, Work!" He's seen what has happened to some of his friends; it seems to him they have no life.

Set the simulation as shown below and then **Run**.

Slider	Setting
Personal drive	0 (none)
Time to adjust participation	1 week
Limit on what you can do	40 hours/week
Hours spent on exercise per week	5 hours/week
Hours spent sleeping per week	70 hours/week

Record your results on the graphs below. Make sure to create labels and a key for each graph. Note that you'll need to click the bottom-left corner of the graph to see Page 2.

Participation in activities and Energy level

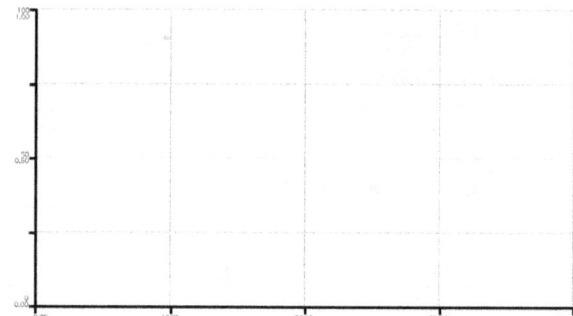

Accomplishments per week, Desired accomplishments per week, and Satisfaction with accomplishments

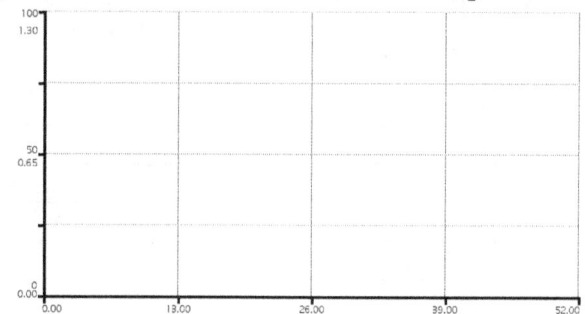

What is happening in the graphs and why?

_____
_____
_____
_____
_____
_____
_____
_____
_____
_____
_____
_____
_____
_____
_____
_____
_____
_____
_____
_____

a. Why do you think Oxford is not experiencing cycles of burnout?
_____
_____
_____

b. Oxford wants to increase his accomplishments, but not by exhausting himself. What are some ideas that would help him increase success while still preventing burnout cycles?
_____
_____
_____

Continue running the simulation, trying different plans for Oxford. Record the graphs for your best run below.

Participation in activities and Energy level

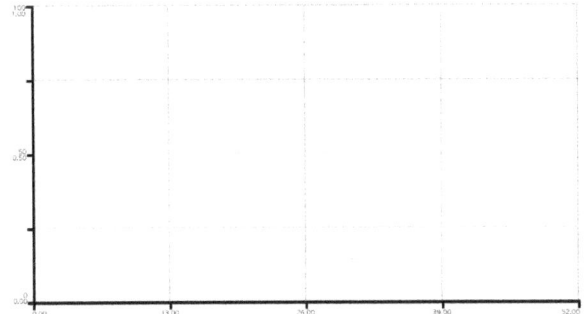

Accomplishments per week, Desired accomplishments per week, and Satisfaction with accomplishments

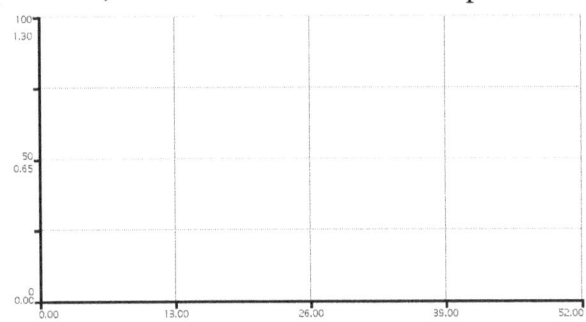

c. What are the new settings?

Slider	Setting
Personal drive	
Time to adjust participation	
Limit on what you can do	
Hours spent on exercise per week	
Hours spent sleeping per week	

d. What changes would Oxford really need to make in his life in order to accomplish this?

_____
_____
_____
_____
_____
_____
_____
_____

LESSON 6, LEVEL C, HANDOUT 2 – P.9

My Pattern
What's your story?
_____
_____
_____
_____
_____

Set the simulation based on your story and record the settings.

Slider	Setting
Personal drive	
Time to adjust participation	week(s)
Limit on what you can do	hours/week
Hours spent on exercise per week	hours/week
Hours spent sleeping per week	hours/week

Record your results on the graphs below. Make sure to create labels and a key for each graph. Note that you'll need to click the bottom-left corner of the graph to see Page 2.

Participation in activities and Energy level

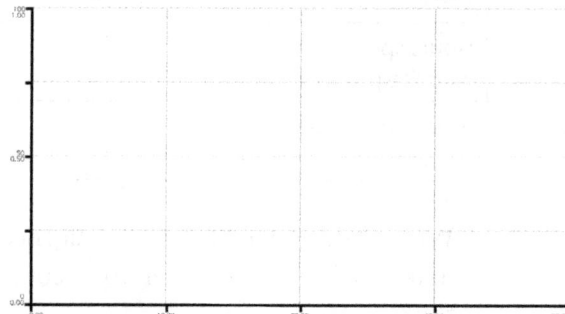

Accomplishments per week, Desired accomplishments per week, and Satisfaction with accomplishments

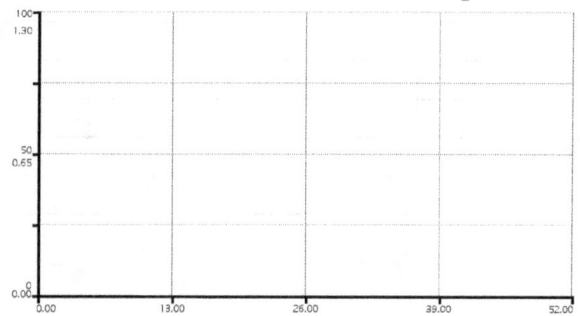

What is happening in the graphs and why?
_____
_____
_____
_____
_____
_____
_____
_____
_____
_____
_____
_____
_____
_____
_____
_____
_____
_____
_____
_____

LESSON 6, LEVEL C, HANDOUT 2 – P.10

a. What's happening on your graphs? Are cycles of burnout happening?
_____
_____
_____

b. How accurate are the graphs in comparison to what's really happening in your life?
_____
_____
_____

c. What, if any, changes would you like to see? If none, please explain why. Try some different ideas using the simulation and then record your favorite run below.
_____
_____
_____
_____
_____
_____

Participation in activities and Energy level

Accomplishments per week, Desired accomplishments per week, and Satisfaction with accomplishments

d. What are the new settings?

Slider	Setting
Personal drive	
Time to adjust participation	
Limit on what you can do	
Hours spent on exercise per week	
Hours spent sleeping per week	

e. What changes would you really need to make in your life in order to accomplish this?
_____
_____
_____
_____
_____
_____

LESSON 6, LEVEL C, HANDOUT 3 – P.1

The Big Squeeze – Debrief

Click Menu.
Click 3. Debrief Central. You'll go through each of these sections of the debrief to process what you experienced in the simulation.

Click A. Behavior Patterns.
Read "The Classic Case" and click What's really happening.
a. When does satisfaction first start to decrease significantly? _____
_____

b. Why is this happening? Use the graphs to explain your answer. _____
_____
_____

c. If you are dissatisfied with your progress, (learning something new, doing well in a sport, e.g.), does that boost your energy or sap it? _____
_____
_____

d. Why isn't this an ideal situation for the mental and physical health of the person? _____
_____
_____

Continue by clicking Back to "The Classic Case" and then Continue.
Read through each of the other four scenarios and then answer the following:
e. Which scenario best slows down the burnout cycles? Why? _____
_____
_____

f. Which scenario would you select as the best option for a person who wants to achieve a lot, but who also wants to avoid burnout? Why? _____
_____

g. How might having a big difference (gap) between what people want to accomplish and what is actually accomplished affect their beliefs about themselves? _____
_____
_____

h. Which pattern is closest to your own? In what way? _____
_____
_____

Click Menu and B. Explore the Model.
Look at the simplified map of the system.
a. How do the three main parts (participation, energy, and accomplishments) affect one another?
_____
_____
_____
_____
_____
_____

Click Tour the Model Structure – Parts 1 and 2. Use the space bar to see one piece added at a time.
b. Looking at the map of the system, fill in the following table.

Stock	What increases the stock?	What decreases the stock?	How does this stock affect another stock(s)?
Participation in activities			
Energy level			
Desired accomplishments			

Click Tour the Loops. **Click** on the B (Balancing) symbols for the explanations. **Click** "More Loops" and read through the explanations of the R (Reinforcing) symbols.

a. Choose one of the loops, draw it here, and "tell the story" of that loop in your own words.

b. How does that loop relate to the behaviors you saw in the simulation?
_____
_____
_____
_____
_____
_____

From "More Loops," **Click** "Back" twice to get to the Debrief Menu and then **click** on **C. Connections.**

a. What three categories relate to the causes of burnout?
_____
_____
_____

b. Which category most strongly relates to your own pattern? In what way?
_____
_____
_____

c. In your own life, what gives you balance? What steps do you take to deal with stress?
_____
_____
_____

LESSON 6, LEVEL C, HANDOUT 4 – P.1

The Big Squeeze – Daily Report

DATE:

TO: Mrs. Darcy, Head Advisor

FROM:

REGARDING: Peer Coaching Session Report

Actions in the simulation that best led to high accomplishments, high satisfaction and low burnout issues (copy your best settings/graphs and explain why):

_____
_____
_____
_____
_____
_____
_____

Participation in activities and Energy level

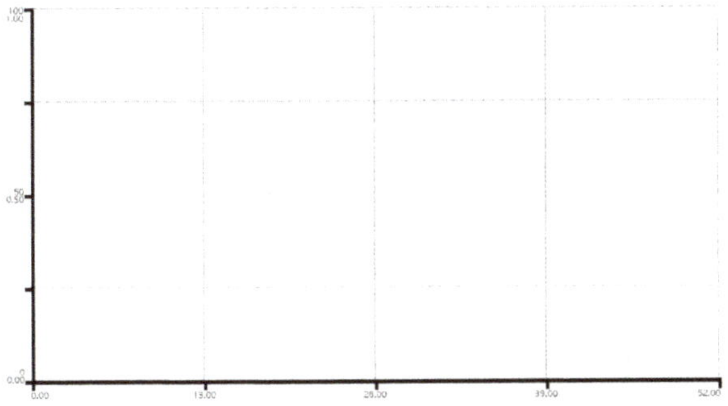

Accomplishments per week, Desired accomplishments per week, and Satisfaction with accomplishments

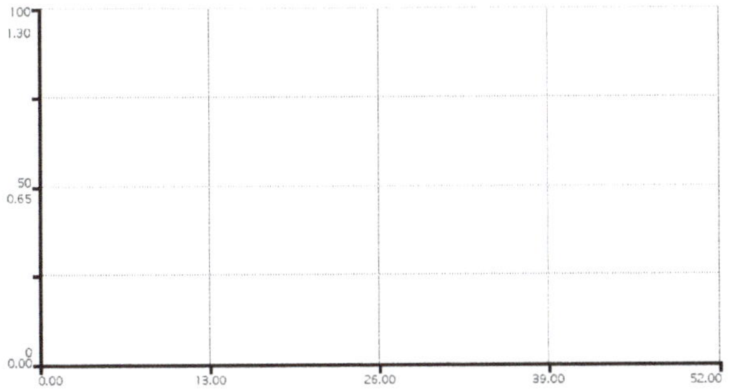

What are the new settings?

Slider	Setting
Personal drive	
Time to adjust participation	
Limit on what you can do	
Hours spent on exercise per week	
Hours spent sleeping per week	

Why did this work?

_____
_____
_____
_____
_____
_____

©2014 Creative Learning Exchange — LESSON 6 – Level C • The Big Squeeze • 115

LESSON 6, LEVEL C, HANDOUT 4 – P.2

Log of Peer Coaching Sessions

Student	Recommendations	Rationale (include proof and examples)
Student #1 – Raven		
Student #2 – Sammy		
Student #3 – Evelyn		
Student #4 – Oxford		

Summary and General Conclusions: (Attach additional supporting documents)

Lesson 7 – Level C

Hog Wild: Fluctuations in Commodities Markets

Overview

This model illustrates how a commodity often oscillates over time, based on supply, demand, and price. Students explore a pork commodity, comparing simulation results given two scenarios for large and small farms.

Learning Goals

- Represent and interpret data on a line graph.
- Identify producers (the supply side) and consumers (the demand side) in the model.
- Articulate the role of price in a marketplace.
- Explain what happens to price when the supply is low and how that affects producers.
- Illustrate the path to market for a commodity.
- Compare large-scale farming to small-scale farming in terms of impact and practicality.

LESSON 7 – LEVEL C – AGES 13+

Time
Three to four 45-minute sessions

Materials
- One computer for every 2–3 students
- Handouts (See pages 121–132)

Curricular Connections
- Math: Vary assumptions, explore consequences, and compare predictions with data.*
- National Curriculum Standards for Social Studies: How people organize for the production, distribution, and consumption of goods and services; scarcity of resources; and economic needs versus wants.
- Economics: Prices send signals and provide incentives to buyers and sellers.

Common Core State Standards

Key system dynamics concepts and insights
- Interdependencies exist among inventory, demand, and price and tend to create oscillations over time.
- Delays are inherent in adjusting supply of a commodity.

Additional information

FIGURE 1: Title Screen

Student Challenge

As a journalist writing for the local newspaper, investigate small versus large-scale farming practices and report on the impact and practicality of different methods.

Lesson Details

Preparation

1. Create groups of 2–3 students each.
2. Check computers to make sure you can access the online simulation.
3. Copy each handout double-sided for each student. See the chart below to determine how many copies of each handout you'll need.

#	Page	Handout	Description
1	121–122	Introduction	This section includes instructions for assembling a learning portfolio and an assessment rubric. Students then get started on the simulation using step-by-step directions.
2	123–128	Scenario Runs	Students experience two farming scenarios and then create their own "hybrid" farm.
3	129–131	Debrief	Students step through the debrief components to reflect on simulation trends and structures.
4	132	Commodity Comparison	After completing the comparison, students write an article.

4. *Optional:* You may want to read the background information about the underlying structure of the model. This can be useful as you guide students to understand the model behavior as it relates to real-world behaviors and the limitations of the model. (Hog Wild Model Background Info available as a separate file http://www.clexchange.org/ftp/documents/x-curricular/CC2012_Oscillations7BackgroundInformation.pdf)

Lesson Sequence

1. Introduce students to any specific content knowledge related to commodities that you'd like them to have prior to running the simulation. This may include definitions of terms such as commodity, supply, demand, inventory, production, distribution, and price.
2. Have students open the simulation and work through the simulation introduction, runs, and debrief using the guided handouts. Note that the handouts guide students through the simulation in a step-by-step manner. If you'd like to leave the exploration more open, then you may eliminate some of the handouts. Figure 2 shows the control panel screen.

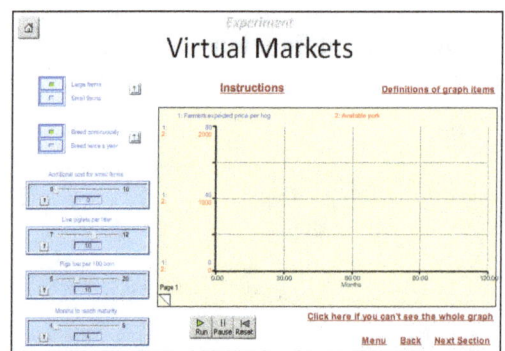

FIGURE 2: Control Panel

Debrief and Assessment

1. Using the instructions and rubric, have students assemble their portfolios and write their articles. Note that a number of additional resources are available for students to research in the Learn More section on the debrief screen.
2. One additional option is to ask students to create a presentation of their findings. Peers could ask questions and give feedback to one another using aspects of the same rubric.
3. Debrief the simulation experience as a class, using ideas for bringing the lesson home.

Bringing the Lesson Home

Discuss these and any other questions/topics that have surfaced about model behaviors.

- What causes fluctuations in price, supply, and demand for a commodity?
- How do decisions about the production and distribution of products affect scarcity?
- What is the role of advertising in food production systems?
- What are the benefits and tradeoffs of farming on a large scale compared to a small scale?
- What determines whether or not a food production system is considered good or bad?
- What are the benefits and tradeoffs of raising a single breed of pig, the "domestic pig," versus rarer heritage breeds?
- How do views about animal rights vary around the world?

Assessment Ideas

Using a rubric, students assemble a portfolio and write an article describing their findings and implications.

ACKNOWLEDGEMENTS

Lesson 7 – Hog Wild: Fluctuations in Commodities Markets • Level C ©2014 Creative Learning Exchange

This model is one in a series of models that explores complex systems and the behaviors produced.

Model created with contributions from Jennifer Andersen, Anne LaVigne, Mike Radzicki, George Richardson, Lees Stuntz, with support from Jay Forrester and the Creative Learning Exchange.

Image Sources and Credits:

Public domain:
Boar - Source: http://commons.wikimedia.org/wiki/File:Landrace_Boar.JPG; author Dingar
Hogs in barn - Source: http://commons.wikimedia.org/wiki/File:Hog_confinement_barn_interior.jpg; author unknown
Mensa connections - Source: http://commons.wikimedia.org/wiki/File:Mensa_Connections.JPG; author Fitzftz
Piglets standing - Source: http://commons.wikimedia.org/wiki/File:Piglets_USDA.jpg; author USDA
Pork - Source: http://commons.wikimedia.org/wiki/File:Pork.jpg; author Guanaco; USDA photo
Wheat - Source: http://commons.wikimedia.org/wiki/File:WheatPennsylvania1943.jpg; author John Collier

The following image is used under the Creative Commons Attribution-ShareAlike 3.0 license (http://creativecommons.org/licenses/by-sa/3.0/) on either Wikipedia.org or Wikimedia Commons:
Coal cars - Source: http://commons.wikimedia.org/wiki/File:Ashtabulacoalcars_e2.jpg; author Decumanus

The following images are used under the Creative Commons Attribution-ShareAlike 3.0 Unported license (http://creativecommons.org/licenses/by-sa/3.0/deed.en) on either Wikipedia.org or Wikimedia Commons:
Coffee beans - Source: http://en.wikipedia.org/wiki/File:Coffee_Beans_Photographed_in_Macro.jpg; author Robert Knapp
Earth - Source: http://commons.wikimedia.org/wiki/File:Earths.jpg; author Stephen Slade Tien
FAO food price index - Source: http://commons.wikimedia.org/wiki/File:FAO_Food_Price_Index.png; author Jashuah, with data from Food and Agricultural Organization of the United Nations
Four sows - Source: http://commons.wikimedia.org/wiki/File:XN_Sus_domesticus_Animal_husbandry_912.jpg; author Guido Gerding
Gold bar - Source: http://en.wikipedia.org/wiki/File:Toi_250kg_gold_bar.jpg; author PHGCOM
Piglets nursing - Source: http://commons.wikimedia.org/wiki/File:Prosiaczki.jpg; author Gumolek
Pumpjack - Source: http://commons.wikimedia.org/wiki/File:Pumpjack_0154.jpg; author Michael C. Rygel

The following image is used under the Creative Commons Attribution-Share Alike 2.5 Generic license (http://creativecommons.org/licenses/by-sa/2.5/deed.en) on either Wikipedia or Wikimedia Commons:
Internet sign - Source: http://commons.wikimedia.org/wiki/File:Internet-Sign.jpg; author cawi2001

The following images are used under the Creative Commons Attribution 2.0 Generic license (http://creativecommons.org/licenses/by/2.0/deed.en) on either Wikipedia.org or Wikimedia Commons:
Large black pigs - Source: http://en.wikipedia.org/wiki/File:Large_Black_pigs.jpg; author Amanda Slater
Sow with piglets - Source: http://en.wikipedia.org/wiki/File:Oregon_State_Fair_pigs.jpg; author Kevin Noone
Title page pig farm - Source: http://commons.wikimedia.org/wiki/File:Pigs_in_hoop_house,_Polyface_Farm.jpg; author Brian Johnson & Dane Kantner
Vegetables - Source: http://en.wikipedia.org/wiki/File:Clagett_Farm_CSA_Week_11.jpg; author thebittenword.com

Other Credits:

National Curriculum Standards for Social Studies, National Council for Social Studies. 2010.
Council for Economic Education, http://www.councilforeconed.org

Hog Wild – Introduction

You are a journalist for the local newspaper. Your assignment is to report on the local pork industry. In preparation for writing the article, you will compare some methods used on small and large farms. You'll explore the simulation sections (in bold) as indicated. Remember, you can always revisit a section anytime you like. Keep in mind that this topic is much more complex than the results within the simulation. You can explore the topic further using the additional resources section before writing your article.

The newspaper's editor, Mr. Wright, will score your article and research portfolio with a rubric (see below). At the conclusion of this project, you will need the following, organized into a portfolio.

1. Your 800–1200 word article for the "Smithtown Daily Herald"
   - Article title
   - Your name as the article's author
   - One or more related illustrations for your article that show parts of the system and how they are connected
2. Handouts 1–4, complete and organized neatly in order
   - Handout 1 – Introduction, Rubric, and Instructions
   - Handout 2 – Scenario Runs
   - Handout 3 – Debrief
   - Handout 4 – Commodity Comparison

Project Assessment Rubric

	Novice	Basic	Proficient	Advanced
Article	Little to no explanation of the data is included. Comparison is non-existent or very confusing.	Some explanation of the data is included, but it includes little detail and has some inaccuracies. Comparison is somewhat unclear and/or incomplete.	Explanations are clear and directly link to the data on the graphs. A clear comparison between the two farm types and effects on the commodity, farmers, and consumers are included.	In addition, the article describes interconnections among the trends that directly impact the commodity, farmers, and consumers over time.
Article Illustration	No illustration is included.	Illustration is included, but it is not clearly linked to the system.	Illustration clearly show key aspects of the system.	In addition, the illustration clearly shows cause-and-effect relationships.
Data and Explanations (within the simulation handouts)	Little to no data is included.	Some data is included, but it is not clear or accurately recorded. Minimal explanations of results are included.	The recorded data is relevant, accurate and clearly represented. Explanations are included that link graph results to logical conclusions.	In addition, the data includes clear connections and explanations among results seen on different graphs.

Open the *Hog Wild: Fluctuations in Commodity Markets-Level C* simulation at http://www.clexchange.org/curriculum/complexsystems/oscillation/oscillation_commoditiesC.asp and **click** "Start."

Click 1. Introduction – Hog Farming

Read the introduction. **Click** and read all the sections on this page. Then answer the following:

a. Define piglet, pig, hog, gilt, sow, and boar.
_____
_____
_____

b. What are your initial thoughts about why the number of customers at farmers' markets is growing?
_____
_____
_____

c. Describe your role as a journalist.
_____
_____
_____

Click Menu.
Click 2. Experiment with the Model

Click the question marks (**?**) for the buttons and slidebars and write definitions in your own words.

Large vs. small farms: _____
_____

Breeding continuously vs. breeding twice a year: _____
_____

Additional cost for small farms: _____
_____

Live piglets per litter: _____
_____

Pigs lost per 100 born: _____
_____

Months to reach maturity: _____
_____

LESSON 7, LEVEL C, HANDOUT 2 – P.1

Hog Wild – Scenario Runs

Scenario #1 – Large Farms

a. Given the settings below, what do you predict will happen to the farmers expected price per hog and the available pork over time?

_____
_____
_____

b. Set the simulation as shown below and then run.

Decision	Setting
Type of farm	large
Breeding plan	breed continuously
Additional cost for small farms	$ 0
Live piglets per litter	10 piglets
Pigs lost per 100 born	10 pigs
Months to reach maturity	4 months

c. Record your results on the graphs below. **Click** on the bottom-left corner of the graph to see Page 2. Make sure to create labels and a key.

Farmers expected price per hog
and Available pork

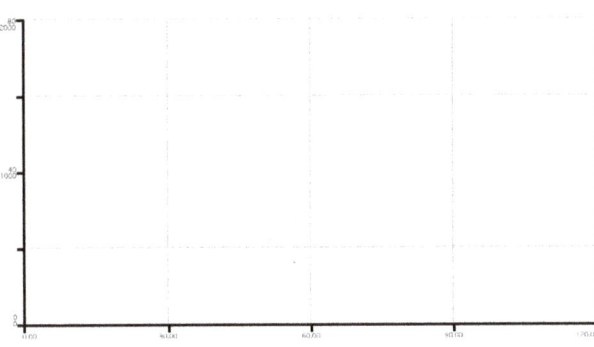

Retail pork price and
Pork eaten per person per month

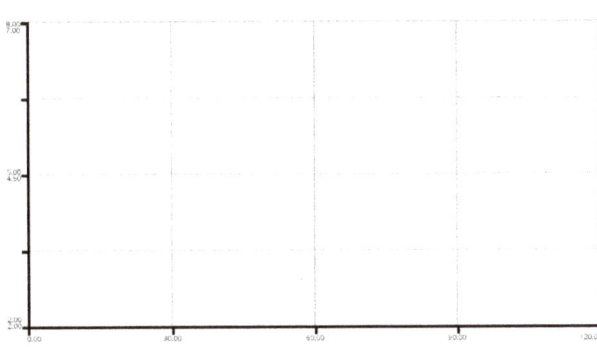

©2014 Creative Learning Exchange

LESSON 7, LEVEL C, HANDOUT 2 – P.2

d. What do you notice about the graphs' trends?

_____
_____
_____
_____

e. Why do you think this occurred? Include specific information about how the large farm settings affected the situation.

_____
_____
_____
_____
_____
_____
_____

Click on the bottom-left corner of the graph to see Page 3.

f. What happened to the number of piglets and mature hogs over time?

_____
_____
_____
_____

g. How do these graphs relate to the retail pork price and the amount of pork eaten per person per month graphs?

_____
_____
_____
_____

Click on the bottom-left corner of the graph to see Page 4.

h. Did the farmers make a profit on the sale of pork over time? Explain why. Notice that the breakeven line shows zero profit. Above that line is a profit, and below the line is a loss.

_____
_____
_____
_____

LESSON 7, LEVEL C, HANDOUT 2 – P.3

Scenario #2 – Small Farms

a. Given the settings below, what do you predict will happen to the farmers' expected price per hog and the available pork over time?
_____
_____
_____

b. Set the simulation as shown below and then run.

Decision	Setting
Type of farm	small
Breeding plan	breed twice a year
Additional cost for small farms	$ 10
Live piglets per litter	7 piglets
Pigs lost per 100 born	20 pigs
Months to reach maturity	8 months

c. Record your results on the graphs below. **Click** on the bottom-left corner of the graph to see Page 2. Make sure to create labels and a key for each graph.

Farmers expected price per hog
and Available pork

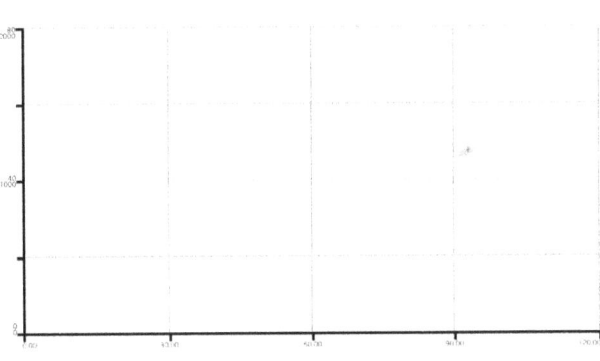

Retail pork price and
Pork eaten per person per month

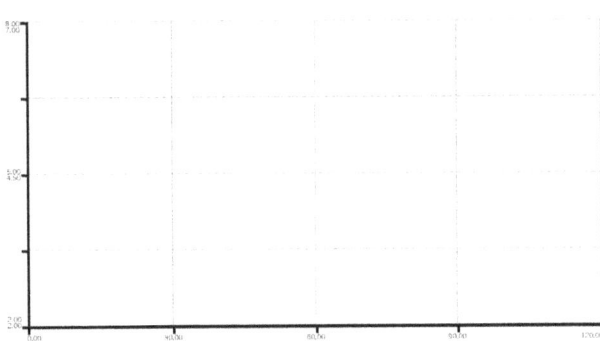

©2014 Creative Learning Exchange

d. What do you notice about the graphs' trends?

_____
_____
_____
_____
_____

e. Why do you think this occurred? Include specific information about how the small farm settings affected the situation.

_____
_____
_____
_____
_____
_____
_____

Click on the bottom-left corner of the graph to see Page 3.
f. What happened to the number of piglets and mature hogs over time?

_____
_____
_____
_____

g. How do these graphs relate to the retail pork price and the amount of pork eaten per person per month graphs?

_____
_____
_____
_____

Click on the bottom-left corner of the graph to see Page 4.
h. Did the farmers make a profit on the sale of pork over time? Explain why.

_____
_____
_____
_____
_____

Scenario #3 – Design a Farm

a. Now it's your turn to set up a farm. You can set up the simulation however you'd like, but consider whether the settings will work in real life. Write a short paragraph describing aspects of the farm.
Description:
_____
_____
_____

b. Set up the simulation, record your settings, make a prediction about what will happen, and then run.

Prediction:

Decision	Setting
Type of farm	
Breeding plan	
Piglets per litter	
Pigs that die per 100	
Extra cost per hog	
Time to raise	

c. Record your results on the graphs below. Make sure to create labels and a key for each graph.

Farmers expected price per hog and Available pork

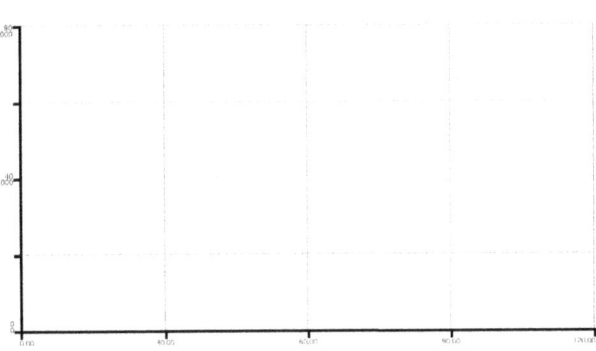

Retail pork price and Pork eaten per person per month

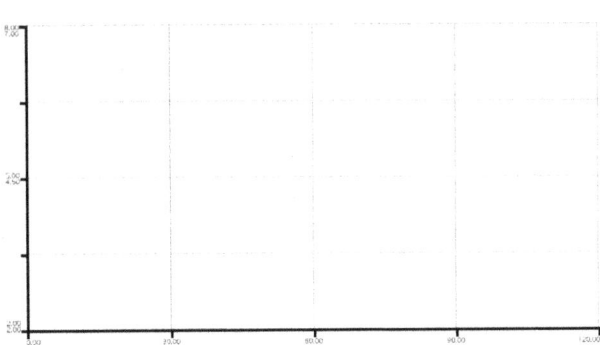

d. What do you notice about the graphs' trends?

_____
_____
_____
_____

e. Why do you think this occurred? Include specific information about how your farm settings affected the situation.

_____
_____
_____
_____
_____
_____
_____

Click on the bottom-left corner of the graph to see Page 3.

f. What happened to the number of piglets and mature hogs over time?

_____
_____
_____
_____

g. How do these graphs relate to the retail pork price and the amount of pork eaten per person per month graphs?

_____
_____
_____
_____

Click on the bottom-left corner of the graph to see Page 4.

h. Did the farmers make a profit on the sale of pork over time? Explain why.

_____
_____
_____
_____

Hog Wild – Debrief

Click Menu. **Click 3. Debrief Central.** You'll go through each of these sections of the debrief to process what you experienced in the simulation.

Click A. Behavior Patterns. Read "Large Farms and Cycles."
a. Looking at the lines on the graph, why do you think farmers on large farms experience cycles in the expected price for their hogs?

_____
_____
_____

b. Why would the availability of pork seem to "follow" what price farmers think they will receive for their hogs? For example, if the price goes up, then so does the availability.

_____
_____
_____

Click and read What's really happening.
c. Draw a diagram to show relationships among supply of pork, demand for pork, and price of pork.

_____
_____
_____

Click Back and Continue. Read "Trying to Keep Up."
d. Looking at the lines on the graph and the settings, why do you think the cycles become larger over time?

_____
_____
_____

Click and read What's really happening.
e. Why do you think it takes longer for farmers to bring down the inventory of pigs than it does for people to change their eating habits?

_____
_____
_____

Click Back and Continue. Read Small Farms and Growth.
f. Why do you think the lines on this graph look very different from the previous graphs?

_____
_____
_____

LESSON 7, LEVEL C, HANDOUT 3 – P.2

Click and read What's really happening.
g. What is your understanding of why the small farms are not experiencing the "wild" ups and downs?
_____
_____
_____

Click Back and Continue. Read "Immune to the Ups and Downs?" and What's really happening?
h. Why does higher efficiency create more extreme ups and downs in a market like hog farming?
_____
_____
_____

Click Back. **Click** Menu and **B. Explore the Model.**
Look at the simplified representation of the system and click on the different parts.
a. What "story" does the diagram tell?
_____
_____
_____
_____

Click Tour the Model Structure and click through each of the parts. Use the space bar to see one piece added at a time.
b. Looking at the map of the system, fill in the following table.

Stock	What increases the stock?	What decreases the stock?	How does this stock affect another stock(s)?
Piglets			
Available pork			
Farmers' expected price for hogs			

130 • LESSON 7 – Level C • Hog Wild ©2014 Creative Learning Exchange

LESSON 7, LEVEL C, HANDOUT 3 – P.3

Click Back. **Click** Tour the Loops. **Click** on the two B (Balancing) and one R (Reinforcing) symbols for the explanations.

c. Choose one of the loops, draw it here, and "tell the story" of that loop in your own words.

_____
_____
_____
_____
_____
_____
_____
_____
_____
_____

d. How does that loop relate to the behaviors you saw in the simulation?

_____
_____
_____

Click Back, Menu and **C. Connections.** Read "A Familiar Story," then **click** Continue and read "Commodities are Everywhere."

a. List at least five examples of commodities that you use.

Commodity	My Use

Click Continue and read "Worldwide Impact."

b. List at least three issues that are a result of commodity price swings.

_____
_____
_____

c. In your own words, what is a price index and how might it be useful?

_____
_____
_____

Hog Wild – Commodity Comparison

Commodity Comparison (Use a separate piece of paper if needed.)

Aspect	Large Farms	Small Farms
Size of farm		
Price fluctuation and impact on the farmers		
Total pork supply (market share)		
Practicality in terms of feeding people		
Community benefits		
Community costs		
Environmental impact in terms of feed sources, topsoil, and waste products		
Treatment of animals		

Everything Else

"You can't navigate well in an interconnected, feedback-dominated world unless you take your eyes off short-term events and look for long-term behavior and structure...."

Donella Meadows, *Thinking in Systems*

PHOTO BY ANNE LAVIGNE

Appendix A
Characteristics of Complex Systems

> "The intuitively obvious 'solutions' to social problems are apt to
> fall into one of several traps set by the character of complex systems."
>
> Jay W. Forrester, *World Dynamics*

Complex systems do not always act the way that people intuit. One way to understand the behaviors of these systems is to view them through a lens of common characteristics. Jay Forrester, MIT professor, developed and described these characteristics, given many years of exploring and modeling a variety of complex systems. His statement summarizes the importance of understanding these characteristics when working to address difficult social issues.

What are the characteristics of complex systems? Forrester described seven distinct characteristics (listed here along with additional explanations). The simulations, along with their accompanying materials, most closely demonstrate characteristic #4, although additional characteristics are also strongly embedded in some of the contexts.

Characteristics of Complex Systems

1. Cause and effect are not closely related in time or space.
Complex systems are composed of many interacting feedback loops. They often contain long time delays. What may appear to be an obvious reason for a particular problem is often not the fundamental cause of the problem, but only a symptom.

2. Action is often ineffective due to application of low-leverage policies.
Complex systems contain balancing feedback loops that surround the various goals of the system. Low-leverage policies often seem to be the "obvious" solutions to the problem at hand, but they encounter resistance – the tendency for interventions to be defeated by the response of the system to the intervention. Low-leverage policies are unable to overpower the balancing loops in order to align the competing goals of the system. In this complex system, the symptoms are commonly treated, rather than the problem.

3. High-leverage policies are difficult to apply correctly.
Complex systems contain areas of high leverage – places where a small push in the correct direction is likely to effect the desired change. In many cases, these high-leverage policies are difficult to identify and difficult to apply correctly. The "levers" for such policies may be pushed in the wrong direction, or not pushed at all.

4. The cause of the problem is within the system.
Problems observed in complex systems are almost always internally generated. While it is easier and more comfortable to place blame on others, it is more productive to look within the system itself to understand and change undesirable behavior. This complex system characteristic is often identified by the oscillation of the system.

5. Collapsing goals results in a downward spiral.
Complex systems tend to drift to lower levels of performance over time. This can occur over a long time-frame, making the downward spiral both insidious and hard to combat. This situation occurs when individuals or institutions respond to failing to reach their goals by adjusting them downward in order to relieve the discomfort of failure.

6. Conflicts arise between short-term and long-term goals.
In complex systems, there are tradeoffs between short-term and long-term goals. What is achievable or desirable within a short time-frame can reveal problematic consequences in the fullness of time. Conversely, concentrating on a future payoff almost always involves sacrifice in the present.

7. Burdens are shifted to the intervener.
This characteristic is often closely related to the tradeoff between short-term and long-term goals. Both play out over time, but the presence of an intervener usually means that a form of addiction or dependence is at work. The system's natural ability to fend for itself declines over time as the addiction/dependence becomes stronger.

Appendix B
System Dynamics Visual Tools

Behavior-over-time Graph

The variable being measured is always on the y-axis of the graph. Time is displayed on the x-axis. Depending on the context, the time frame could be short (measured in seconds) or long (measured in years). Most of the models in this series produce a variety of oscillatory behaviors, although other trends are also possible.

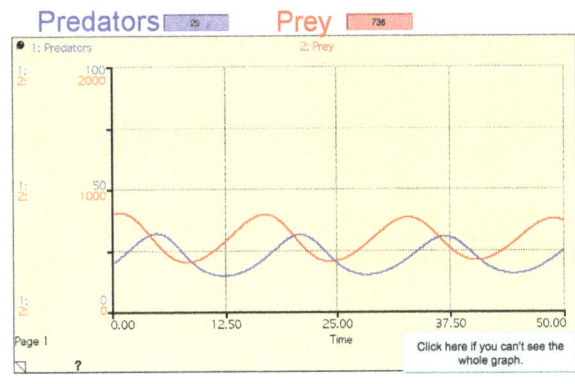

Causal Loop Diagram

A causal (or feedback) loop diagram is another visual tool that shows the structure of a system. A feedback loop tells a story about how a system operates. Any given system may have multiple interconnected loops. Arrows between any two elements indicate a cause-and-effect relationship: If the first element rises, then it causes the second element either to rise or fall. Depending on the relationship, different symbols are used. See the loop below along with the key explaining the different symbols.

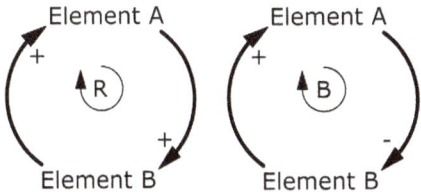

+ indicates a direct or additive relationship between the two elements.
- indicates an indirect or subtractive relationship between the two elements.
R in the middle indicates that the loop reinforces.
B in the middle indicates that the loop balances.

Stock/Flow Map

A stock/flow map represents the structure of the system. The parts of the map along with the underlying mathematical assumptions define the nature of the interdependent relationships among the parts. This structure is based on assumptions about how the system (whether it be a spring or relationships on the playground) really works.

In its simplest form, a stock represents an accumulated amount and the flow (or flows) represent the rate at which the stock goes up or down. Other elements impact one or more flows, either adding to or subtracting from a stock.

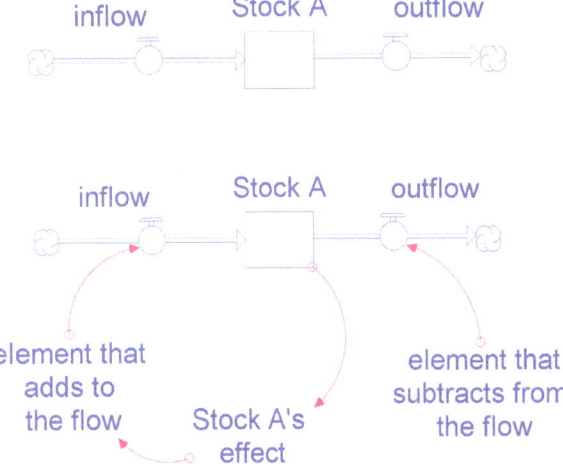

©2014 Creative Learning Exchange

Appendix C
Technical Matters

Setting Up the Simulation

Menu System

Each simulation level has a standardized menu system displayed in a recommended order of use. Handouts guide students through all sections of each level's menu system.

Level A Menu

Level B Menu

| Introduction | Decisions | Simulation Results | Debrief | Next Steps |

Level C Menu Example

1. Introduction – Spring Dynamics
2. Experiment with the Model
3. Debrief Central – Expand your Knowledge
    A. Behavior Patterns
    B. Explore the Model
    C. Connections
    D. Learn More – Additional Resources

Home

 Every screen has a "Home" button available. This button returns the user to the beginning title screen of the simulation.

Slidebars

Slidebars are one method for manipulating the settings for a simulation. Some of the slidebars have a general range, with no values showing. One example within the Level A – Spring Simulation shows a range of springiness from "easy to pull" to "hard to pull." Other simulations have slidebars that include numerical settings. The lesson handouts might ask the student to set a slidebar to a particular number.

General Range Slidebar   **Specific Numerical Slidebar**

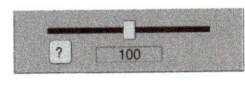

Initial position

Additional aspects of slidebars include:
- Setting a slidebar is as simple as moving the lever to the right or left to select higher or lower settings.
- Slidebars that have visible numerical values can also be set by clicking on the value in the middle and typing in the desired number.
- Slidebars must be set according the indicated minimum and maximum values. For example, if a range is 0–2000, the user will not be able to type in a value that exceeds 2000.
- Slidebars must be set by certain increments, depending on the variable. For example, if a range is 0–2000, then the increments may go up or down by increments of 100.

Knobs

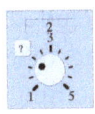 Some of the Level C simulations contain one or more knobs on the control panel screen. These have minimum and maximum values and are set by moving the black dot around to the desired setting.

Buttons

Buttons are used throughout a simulation for different purposes, including navigation among the pages of the simulation, initiating a new simulation run, and resetting the simulation graphs. Depending on the level of the simulation, these buttons may be rectangular images or resemble links on a webpage.

Graphs

Graphs show simulation results as a behavior-over-time graph. The simulation lesson handouts for the B and C levels presume that students know how to create, title, label, and create a key for a line graph.

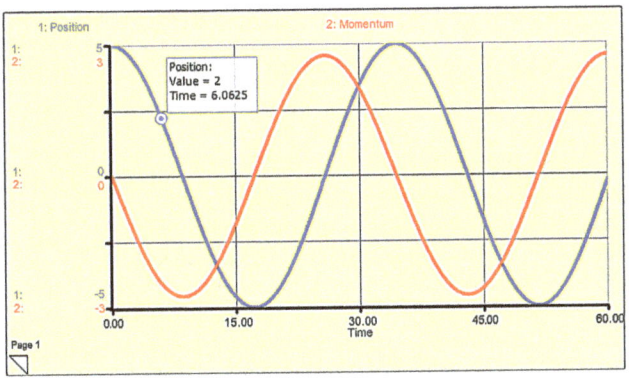

Some graphs may have multiple pages. To see the additional graphs, click on the tab at the bottom, left of the graph pad. Each time you click, the next graph appears. After clicking through all the graphs, the first one will again appear.

To see the actual values at any point on a graph line, click and hold the mouse arrow, right on the line at the point you'd like to check. A box will appear showing the value at a particular point in time.

©2014 Creative Learning Exchange

Troubleshooting

"The simulation gives me a 'time out' message."
When running the simulation online, you may occasionally experience a "time out" message. This can occur for a variety of reasons, but the most common is when nothing on the simulation screen has been clicked for a while. If this happens, simply reload the page and return to the screen you last visited.

"The text and the graphics are all 'mixed up.'"
Occasionally, the development team updates simulations to improve them. If your computer browser has an old version saved in its memory, this can cause the simulation to display erroneous information. To fix this issue, you need to clear the cache from your browser. Browsers (e.g., Internet Explorer, Firefox, Safari) have different procedures for doing this, so see the help documentation for your browser if needed.

"The simulation behavior doesn't make sense."
Each of the simulation models in this series has limitations and is valid only when used within those limitations. If settings that exceed the model parameters are put into the simulation, the user may experience behavior on the graph that doesn't make sense.

For example, the animal population simulation shows the population trends for the animals included on the handouts. If the user tries to input data for an animal that has a very long lifespan and that frequently has many offspring, an exponential growth pattern may be produced. In reality, something else would limit the population growth, but the parameters of the simulation are not able to handle that extreme scenario.

See the accompanying background documents for additional information about the limitations of each model.

"I can't see the entire line on the graph."
In some cases, you may input settings that cause the behavior to go beyond the scale of a particular graph. If this occurs, most of the simulations have a button that allows the user to see the full graph. Note that no scale is set for this special graph, but rather a new scale (on the y-axis) is created with each new run.

"The QR codes are not working."
You can access all the simulations here:
https://exchange.iseesystems.com/profile/25/52

Background documents based on Level C simulations are available here:
Springs- http://static.clexchange.org/ftp/documents/x-curricular/CC2012_Oscillations1BackgroundInformation.pdf
Playground- http://static.clexchange.org/ftp/documents/x-curricular/CC2012_Oscillations2BackgroundInformation.pdf
Population- http://static.clexchange.org/ftp/documents/x-curricular/CC2012_Oscillations3BackgroundInformation.pdf
Pred/prey- http://static.clexchange.org/ftp/documents/x-curricular/CC2012_Oscillations4BackgroundInformation.pdf
Pred/prey/food- http://static.clexchange.org/ftp/documents/x-curricular/CC2012_Oscillations5_BackgroundInformation.pdf
Burnout - http://static.clexchange.org/ftp/documents/x-curricular/CC2012_Oscillations6BackgroundInformation.pdf
Commodities - http://static.clexchange.org/ftp/documents/x-curricular/CC2012_Oscillations7BackgroundInformation.pdf

About Us

About the Authors

Jennifer Andersen is a system dynamics professional who collaborates with the Creative Learning Exchange to create simulations for a wide audience. Since completing her education in simulation modeling fifteen years ago, she has consulted for many projects in the US, Scandinavia, Europe, and South America. She is particularly interested in promoting system dynamics as a tool for understanding complex systems and enhancing formal education in the STEM (Science, Technology, Engineering and Math) disciplines.

Anne LaVigne works with the Creative Learning Exchange and the Waters Foundation. She is a teacher, coach, instructional designer, and most importantly, a learner. For more than twenty years, she has collaborated with educators and students across K-12 settings using systems thinking and system dynamics tools. She strives to develop and share strategies for understanding dynamic, interdependent systems in ways that empower, engage, and motivate.

Lees Stuntz has worked for over twenty years encouraging the use of system dynamics and systems thinking in K-12 education. As Executive Director of the Creative Learning Exchange, she has created and edited multiple pieces of curriculum – available on the Creative Learning Exchange's website (www.clexchange.org), including seven books, as well as numerous curricular units. She collaborates with educators, system dynamicists and citizen advocates toward a collective goal of educating students to be effective systems citizens in our complex world.

The Creative Learning Exchange

The Creative Learning Exchange was founded as a non-profit organization in 1991 to encourage an active, learner-centered process of discovery for 5–19 year-old students that engages in meaningful, real-world problem solving through the mastery of systems thinking and system dynamics modeling. Since its inception, the CLE has worked to encourage teachers and educators to use systems thinking and system dynamics in classrooms and schools throughout the United States, as well as internationally. The CLE has done this through its website that offers free curriculum, its products that include books and games that promote systems thinking, and a biennial conference to help educators and students learn and utilize systems thinking and system dynamics in the classroom and the school organization.

System Dynamics and Jay Forrester

System dynamics is a field of study and a perspective for understanding change. Using computer simulation and other tools, system dynamics looks at how the feedback structure of systems causes the change we observe all around us. System dynamics was developed over fifty years ago by Professor Jay W. Forrester, MIT Professor Emeritus, and is used to address problems in areas ranging from ecology to business management, economics, and psychology. Under Forrester's guidance, system dynamics is helping teachers make K-12 education more learner-centered, engaging, challenging, and relevant to our rapidly changing world.

For more than twenty-five years, Professor Forrester has fostered this work within K-12 education. His direct support allowed the creation of these simulations and accompanying materials, which enables students to explore what are often befuddling characteristics of complex systems.

Led by a partnership between Dr. Forrester and the Creative Learning Exchange, the goal of this ongoing project is to create online curriculum materials for students, aged five and above, to illustrate characteristics of complex systems. In exploring the nature of complex social systems, the materials address questions such as:

- Why do such systems resist policy changes?
- Why are short-term and long-term responses to corrective action often at odds with each other?
- How can leverage points be applied to bring about desirable change in social systems?

The goals of the project are grounded in the belief that an abstract level of understanding of social systems will help prepare future citizens to actively shape their society.

www.ingramcontent.com/pod-product-compliance
Lightning Source LLC
Chambersburg PA
CBHW080557090426
42735CB00016B/3265